# THE ROLLER COASTER ECONOMY

## FINANCIAL CRISIS, GREAT RECESSION, AND THE PUBLIC OPTION

### HOWARD J. SHERMAN

#### WITH JOHN MILLER AND PAUL SHERMAN

*M.E.Sharpe*
Armonk, New York
London, England

Dedicated to Barbara with love.

**Library of Congress Cataloging-in-Publication Data**

Sherman, Howard J.
  The roller coaster economy : financial crisis, great recession, and the public option /
Howard J. Sherman.
     p. cm.
  Includes bibliographical references and index.
  ISBN 978-0-7656-2537-3 (cloth: alk. paper)—ISBN 978-0-7656-2538-0 (pbk.: alk. paper)
  1. Business cycles—United States—History—21st century.  2. Financial crises—United
States—History—21st century.  3. Recessions—United States—History—21st century.
I. Title.

  HB3743.S54 2010
  330.973—dc22                                                                      2009032157

Printed in the United States of America

The paper used in this publication meets the minimum requirements of
American National Standard for Information Sciences
Permanence of Paper for Printed Library Materials,
ANSI Z 39.48-1984.

IBT (c)   10    9    8    7    6    5    4    3    2    1
IBT (p)   10    9    8    7    6    5    4    3    2    1

# THE
# ROLLER COASTER
# ECONOMY

# Contents

# Preface and Acknowledgments

Many beginning textbooks speak as if the U.S. economy usually follows a smooth upward path at full employment, with only occasional wobbles caused by outside shocks to it. This book demonstrates that the normal course of the U.S. economy more closely resembles a roller coaster. At the peak of the roller coaster, those who live on corporate profit do very well, while ordinary folk are barely able to survive and get on with their lives. At the bottom of the roller coaster, however, millions of people are unemployed and miserable, corporate profits disappear, many businesses close their doors, credit is impossible to get, and a great many people lose their homes. This process is repeated over and over for what seem to be mysterious reasons.

Part II of the book concentrates on the deep recession and financial crisis of 2007 to 2009. It avoids presenting a chaotic avalanche of data, rather presenting the story in clear graphs. The graphs present the most important facts for the reader to inspect, including what happened to wages and salaries, housing, corporate profits, and other key variables.

Part III puts together all of facts the reader has learned into a single, coherent story. It explains why the recession occurred, why it was so bad, and why there was a financial crisis. Last, but not least, the book presents the highlights of the policy debate.

It explores how the Obama administration stimulated the economy. Moreover, President Barack Obama argued that the present system of health care is broken and needs drastic change to fix it. He argued for many changes, but his focus was on a public plan as an option for consumers to take if private insurance plans are too expensive or otherwise impossible to obtain.

This book argues, on the basis of an intensive empirical examination, that the present economic system is broken. It requires drastic changes to fix it. This book recommends various reforms, including the need for a public option to provide employment for the unemployed, who cannot get jobs in private enterprises. It considers how the economy may be kept at full employment forever.

Since human beings designed the economic system, there is no reason why humans cannot correct its faults. If the reforms are complete and drastic enough, then crises, recessions, and unemployment can be a thing of the past.

## What the Book Attempts to Do

The book is written in popular language for people with no training in economics. There is no use of the language of statistics or math. Rather, everything in the process of boom and bust is explained in very simple graphs, showing what actually happened, with explanations of the process.

Even economists who disagree with the viewpoint may find the factual description of the recession and the crisis useful for their students. Those who wish to know the statistical approach will find it discussed briefly with full citations in Chapter 3, while the underlying model is discussed briefly in the Appendix to Chapter 11 with citations to sources.

For those who want to know about the stock market, see Appendices 8.2 and 8.3 in Chapter 8.

## Note on the Language

In some situations, it is very awkward to use the terms "U.S." or "United States" to mean the country of or the people of the United States of America. For example, "Americans" is a lot simpler than "citizens of the United States of America." And "U.S. people" sounds too formal. So this book sometimes uses "America" or "Americans" for the land or the people of the United States.

The author is clear that Central Americans and South Americans are also Americans. Therefore, I apologize for this use of "American" to mean only people of the United States of America.

This book is mainly about the United States, including its relations with the global economy. It does not ever focus on Central or South America, so there can be no confusion. The reason it does deal very little with any of the developing countries is that all recessions and depressions originate in the developed capitalist countries. The recession or depression is always given to the underdeveloped countries as a gift. It is a gift that causes even more terrible havoc in the underdeveloped countries than in the developed capitalist countries.

This book would never have been finished without the help of John Miller. He has at his fingertips an enormous amount of current data; and he put much of that data into clear prose in his explanations to me. He corrected my theoretical conceptions on some important points. He directly contributed to three chapters. He has given me moral support whenever I needed it. He has also commented in depth on the entire manuscript.

This book also could not have been written without the contributions of Paul Sherman. He gathered all the data for the graphs, he calculated all of the data for the graphs, and he made the graphs. Since a large part of this book is built around that data and the graphs, it could not have been done without him. Since he is a computer engineer, he does everything at high speed, with accuracy, and with professional attention to its appearance. He also gave me much needed moral support, as well as voluntarily editing much of the book.

Robert Pollin gave me a lengthy set of brilliant insights into my errors. Barbara Sinclair lent me her extensive knowledge of political science to point out both mistakes in fact and exaggeration in the political area. I have tried to fix each of these errors.

Lisa Sherman, who put great effort into the editing process, made an immense improvement.

I also thank Lynn Taylor, executive editor at M.E. Sharpe, for all the effort she expended to make this book a reality.

# Part I

# Problems of the
# Roller Coaster Economy

# 1

# Boom, Bust, and Misery

## The Curse of Capitalism

When Alice was in Wonderland, it was a topsy-turvy place that Alice found very confusing. The present capitalist market economy, much like Alice's Wonderland, often seems topsy-turvy and confusing to most people, perhaps never more so than today.

Right now, as this book is written in 2009, millions of Americans have lost their jobs and go without a secure income. More than 1 million U.S. homeowners are facing foreclosure and the loss of their homes. Thousands of businesses are going bankrupt, mostly small businesses, but also some very large ones.

You might think from these facts that the economy produced too much, hired too many workers, and created too many companies. But millions of people in the United States need more to eat, more clothes, and more shelter. In 2007, more than 37 million people, some 12.5 percent of the U.S. population, lived in poverty without enough money to get by on. Those numbers go up every day as the economy spirals downward.

If so many people urgently need so many things, why does the economy act like it has produced too much? Why do unsold clothes pile up on store shelves, cars sit in showrooms, and houses stand empty, when so many go without?

These same topsy-turvy contradictions appear in the global economy. Economies across the globe—not just the U.S. economy, but also the European, Japanese, and even the red-hot Chinese and Indian economies—are cutting back production. European finance employees, Japanese electronics employees, Chinese garment workers, and Indian software employees are losing their jobs as their economies slow and the world export market dries up.

But there is great need for more production. In 2005, 1.4 billion people, about one-quarter of the population of the developing world, lived in extreme poverty, making do on less than US$1.25 a day. Half the population of sub-Saharan Africa, 380 million people, continues to live in extreme poverty. The poverty-stricken and many others need more food, more clothing, and more shelter.

The world economy has enormous capacity to produce. Instead of producing more, however, economies across the globe are producing less. They are firing their employees.

It is this strange, contradictory, topsy-turvy state of affairs that reminds us of *Alice's Adventures in Wonderland* (Carroll 1901). Alice would find that the economic system reduces production when many people urgently need more goods and services. She would think this is strange and mysterious, and perhaps as topsy-turvy as Wonderland.

## Resolving the Mystery

The first step in solving this mystery is to recognize that the economy has *not* produced more than people need. The economic output is only more than people have the money to buy at a price that yields a profit.

Today's housing and mortgage crisis makes that clear. In the fall of 2008, homelessness reached record levels all across the United States. In Massachusetts in September 2008, for example, 2,000 families lived in shelters. Another 574 families could not find shelter space and were temporarily housed elsewhere. At the same time, 18.6 million housing units in the United States stood empty. U.S. housing prices were down nearly 20 percent from their peak in late 2005. Sales of new homes had just about dried up. And housing starts, the building of new homes, reached their lowest level since record keeping began in 1947. Only in a topsy-turvy world could Massachusetts and every other state scramble to provide shelter to a record number of homeless families while millions of homes lie empty.

For some people, these contradictions are not so bothersome. Take *Wall Street Journal* columnist Holman Jenkins. How would he "shake off the mortgage mess"? That is easy: demolish unoccupied houses. Unsold houses, figures Jenkins, "go rancid on the shelf, souring the values of the nation's entire housing stock," pulling down its price. Destroying unsold houses would, he argues, reduce the supply of housing and drive up housing prices (Jenkins 2008). Jenkins's reasoning is the quintessential example of the market economy's upside-down logic. Jenkins is more obsessed with driving the price of houses back up than with the plight of the homeless. How else could he advocate destroying unoccupied houses to make those

4

that remain on the market more expensive, while many families go without a home?

Unemployment is another example of the topsy-turvy nature of the economy. Employees lose their jobs because the commodities they produce go unsold. But without a job or income, they too will lack the money they need to purchase the goods they badly need. And then yet more employees will lose their jobs. The number of unemployed climbs by millions as the economy produces less and less, and employs fewer and fewer workers and professionals. All the while, the millions of people without jobs would be happy to work to produce the goods that they so desperately need.

How can this strange mystery be solved? This question is of vital importance to people all over the world. This book seeks to unravel the mystery of how vast numbers of people are unemployed while millions of people urgently need more food, clothing, and shelter. This book was written both to explain the mystery and to discuss ways to change this topsy-turvy economy for the better.

**Recession and Depression**

In economic expansions, American production rises while unemployment falls. Every expansion in American history, however, has been followed by an economic contraction. If the contraction is relatively mild by historical standards, it is called a recession. If it is more severe, it is called a depression. The difference can best be explained by a joke first made by President Harry Truman: If your friend loses her job, he said, it is a recession; if you lose your job, it is a depression. When the contraction lasted ten years and official unemployment went up to 25 percent in the 1930s, it was called the Great Depression.

The term "depression" was commonly used before World War II to refer to any economic contraction. From 1948 to 2001, there were ten minor contractions. Conservatives did not like the term "depression" because it reminded everyone of the horrors of the Great Depression which they would rather forget, while denying that the economy had any basic problem. So conservatives invented the term "recession" to convey the idea that the problem was mild and temporary. Eventually the term "recession" was widely used.

Now, in 2009, America is in the most violent contraction since 1929. It is even larger than the recession of 1982, which had been the biggest one since the 1930s. Conservatives want to call it a recession. But that word is not strong enough for most people. Paul Volcker, a past chair of the Federal Reserve System, has called it a "Great Recession" (Volcker 2009, p. 1).

A "Great Recession" reflects actuality a lot better than just the term "recession." The Great Recession of 2007 to 2009 reflected new economic structures that have arisen in the last thirty years and have born a bitter fruit. More people have lost their jobs than in any other contraction since the Great Depression. Although it is not in the same class with the Great Depression, this Great Recession is bigger than any of the previous recessions in many ways. Americans have witnessed a deep contraction with an entirely different quality. An elephant is not just a bigger horse; it is qualitatively different.

Moreover, this contraction represented dramatic changes in the economic structure. The structure of the economy means the building blocks of which it is built and how they fit together. No contraction since the Great Depression has caused such a strong financial crisis. No other recession has seen millions of foreclosures that meant the end of the American dream of owning a house. No other recession has had so many large corporations teetering close to bankruptcy.

But there was also a financial crisis in the middle of the Great Recession. This crisis has been building for decades as the whole economic structure slowly changed. So the most accurate description of the 2007 to 2009 situation would be a Great Recession with a Financial Crisis. That is too big a mouthful, so the book will use the term "Great Recession" for the period 2007 to 2009. The expansion that preceded the Great Recession should be called the expansion of 2001 to 2007 during the Bush administration, but it will be called the Bush expansion for short. Part II of this book will discuss the extent to which the Bush administration influenced the major variables.

Three questions will be explored in this book. First, why did the most recent expansion turn into a Great Recession? Second, what were the structural changes that led to the crisis of 2008? Third, in the last chapter, the question is what to do about it. That is, what changes have to be made in the structure of the U.S. economy to stop this sort of thing from happening ever again?

**The Curse of Unemployment**

In the first half of 2009, unemployment in the United States rose by half a million every month. The auto industry has been especially hard-hit. Of the big three, General Motors (GM) sold the lowest number of vehicles in forty-nine years in 2008. Both GM and Chrysler, the third largest auto company, went bankrupt in 2009. Despite these massive job losses, some politicians and economists in the United States blamed unemployment on the people, rather than the businesses that fired them. Former senator Phil Gramm, a politician with a PhD in economics, said in July 2008 that the United States had "become a nation of whiners" and dismissed the downturn as nothing more than a "mental recession" (see Cooper 2008).

Conservative economic think tanks, such as the Heritage Foundation, insisted that the rising unemployment was not attributable to corporations firing employees. Rather, corporations were creating fewer new jobs because of high taxes. For them, the important way to cure the problem of unemployment was cutting business taxes. There was no need to extend unemployment benefits (see Sherk 2009).

This pro-corporate apology and dismissal of recessions are not new. "Absolutely sound" was President Calvin Coolidge's assessment of the economy and the stock market in 1929. In the fall of 1929, Hoover's secretary of the Treasury, Andrew Mellon, reassured one and all that "there is no cause to worry. The high tide of prosperity will continue." Finally, in mid-October 1929, no less than Irving Fisher, the preeminent U.S. economist of his day, proclaimed that "stock prices have reached what looks like a permanently high plateau" (see Galbraith 1988, pp. 15, 26, 41, and 70).

A few days later the stock market crashed, and the U.S. economy sank into a depression that was to last a decade. By 1933, at least 25 percent of the labor force was unemployed and another 25 percent was on involuntary part-time work or was so discouraged that they gave up looking for jobs. The homeless, the hungry, and the desperate were never fully counted. The most famous pictures of the era showed long lines of people waiting for free bread or a bowl of soup. These breadlines, as they were called, would sometimes extend for blocks from the entrance of a soup kitchen.

Some modern economists still argue that the high wages of employees prevented a normal economic recovery during the Great Depression. As they see it, New Deal policies increased the bargaining power of employees and allowed them to push up their wages and salaries. Those high labor costs kept employers from hiring back employees in the long depression (see Cole and Ohanian 2004, pp. 813–815; see also Spirer, Spirer, and Jaffe 1998, p. 139).

This widespread belief that employees themselves, not the economic system, should shoulder the blame for the Great Depression reduced sympathy for the unemployed. This belief only reinforced the corroding effect that unemployment had on the sense of self-worth of the millions who lost their jobs in the Great Depression. In *Hard Times* (1970), a riveting oral history of the Great Depression, Studs Terkel recorded hundreds of people's recollections of their hard times. Terkel captures the courageous spirit of his subjects. Some of the more articulate and the political rebels attributed their suffering to outside economic forces and worked to change the economy. They did this through hunger marches and protests.

Among the millions of unemployed, however, "the great many were wounded, in one manner or another," writes Terkel. "The suddenly-idle hands blamed themselves, rather than society. Millions experienced a private kind of shame when the pink slip came. No matter that others suffered the same fate, the inner voice whispered, 'I'm a failure'" (Terkel 1970, p. 5). The notion that employees have no one to blame but themselves when they lose their job persists today. Most of the unemployed still bitterly reproach themselves as failures. Most politicians and economists perpetuate this view. When asked about black unemployment in the severe recession of 1982, President Ronald Reagan famously pointed to the help-wanted ads in the *Washington Post*. "I made it a point to count the pages of help-wanted ads," he replied. "In this time of great unemployment, there were 24 full pages of classified ads of employers looking for employees. What we need is to make more people qualified to go and apply for those jobs" (Reagan 1982).

Actually there were twenty-six pages of ads, but most were devoted to job openings for professionals, such as engineers, unlikely to be filled by the unemployed. But even at that, there were only 3,500 jobs advertised, while 85,000 people were unemployed in the metropolitan Washington area at the time (see Spirer, Spirer, and Jaffe 1998, p. 139).

Equally tenacious is the belief that the economy itself is inherently stable and could not be the root cause of an economic collapse. That was Republican presidential candidate John McCain's reaction when the U.S. financial market froze in the fall of 2008. During the Great Recession year of 2008, Senator McCain took to the stump to assure the American people that "the fundamentals of our economy are strong," sounding chillingly like Calvin Coolidge and Herbert Hoover on the eve of the Great Depression. The same day as Senator McCain made his statement, Lehman Brothers, the giant investment bank, declared bankruptcy (Stein 2008).

In spite of recessions and depressions, some conservative economists and politicians still argue that anyone who really tries can get a job, so all unemployment is purely voluntary. Is it true that unemployment is voluntary and the unemployed are personal failures? All the evidence says otherwise. Unemployment is due to the usual way that the institutions of the present capitalist economy operate. The main types of evidence are the following.

First, the reality reported every few days in all U.S. newspapers in 2008 and 2009 was that many firms, not just automobile makers, were firing thousands of people at a time. Citigroup, the giant banking conglomerate, decided to fire 53,000 employees. Alcoa, the aluminum maker, decided to cut 15,000 employees, 13 percent of its worldwide workforce. DHL, the express shipper, decided to get rid of 9,500 employees, 73 percent of its U.S. workforce. Dell computers announced it would fire 8,900 employees, one-tenth of its workforce. Circuit City, the failing electronics retailer, announced it would let go of 8,000 employees, one-fifth of its work force (this is before it went out of business). And many, many more companies could be added to this list.

When corporations fire thousands of employees, from guards to engineers, they do not blame employees for their individual shortcomings. They simply fire them.

Second, in every economic downturn, people look every day at the help-wanted advertisements in the newspapers. At the peak of the cycle in 2007, job ads ran day after day, sometimes with no takers. In a downturn, however, the number of job ads drop precipitously.

Third, the change in employment is systemic, reflecting changes in the aggregate economy. American employees lost jobs each and every month of 2008. All told, 2.6 million Americans lost their jobs in 2008, the highest number in one year since 1945 at the end of World War II.

When jobs disappear month after month and unemployment rises across the country, the fault is not with those who lost their jobs. Rather, the economic system is clearly at fault. When the economy collapses, corporations curtail their demand for labor. They do not hire new employees, they fire them. Employees do not lose their jobs because they become too lazy to work or in order to look for a new job. On the contrary, they lose their jobs because those jobs no longer exist. If 2.6 million employees lost their jobs because of individual failures, they would not all have lost them during 2008. Moreover, if the blame was individual, thousands of employees at one corporation would not lose their jobs at the same time.

In fact, the pattern of the expansion and decline of employment and output in the whole economy is remarkably stable. It reproduces itself business cycle after business cycle. The recession may be faster or slower, shallower or deeper, but, as will be seen in this book, the general patterns of employment and output over the cycle persist. The consistency of these cyclical patterns also is evidence against the view that unemployment is a personal failure and not a failure of the economic system.

If the cycle of boom and bust of the roller coaster economy endlessly repeats itself, what is the cause? This book will reveal that the basic cause is the institutions of capitalism.

Briefly, capitalism is a system of private ownership of enterprises, with profit as its goal. The owners employ material equipment and human beings, who are called employees. The process of production and delivery of goods and services yields a profit to the owners of capital, who are called capitalists.

Production takes place only when capitalists expect to make a profit. When profit declines, capitalists no longer invest. Instead, they curtail production.

This loss of production costs employees their jobs. This scourge of unemployment is inflicted on employees in every recession or depression.

Chapter 3 will show that the amount of unemployment goes down in every capitalist expansion, but goes up again in every capitalist recession. The workings of the economic system with its roller coaster movements cause large-scale unemployment. How the economic system creates unemployment will be explored later in this book.

**Unused Employees: A Closer Look at Unemployment**

Let us begin by looking at exactly how the unemployment rate behaves over the roller coaster of the business cycle. The unemployment rate is the percentage of people without jobs compared to the total labor force. The Bureau of Labor Statistics of the U.S. Department of Labor (www.bls.gov) calculates the unemployment rate by means of a survey that is seasonally adjusted. The official rate of unemployment averaged over the last five business cycles fell by 42 percent in expansions as more employees were hired. The unemployment rate rose an average of 42 percent in the last five recessions as more employees were fired.

The total output and rate of employment of the economy always rise during expansions and fall during recessions. Both series move pro-cyclically, or with the business cycle. But the unemployment rate moves in the opposite direction to employment. The unemployment rate *falls* during expansion, but *rises* in recessions. Its movements are countercyclical, or opposite to the business cycle.

During every expansion, the economy adds more and more production. To produce more, corporations hire more employees, adding to the number of employees in the labor force. As a result, the unemployment rate falls in the expansion. On the other hand, in a contraction more and more employees are fired, so the unemployment rate must rise.

**The Official Unemployment Rate and Its Shortcomings**

In May 2009, the official unemployment rate stood at 9.4 percent, meaning 14 million people were unemployed. That is a lot of unemployed people, but the number was still rising rapidly. The Labor Department's official unemployment rate, however, dramatically understates the extent of unemployment. First, the Bureau of Labor Statistics (BLS) does not count as unemployed any man or woman without a job unless they are still actively looking for work. If a person has become so discouraged that she did not actively look for a job in the previous four weeks, then she is not counted as unemployed. In fact, she is said to have dropped out of the labor force.

Second, the BLS leaves out part-time employees from the count of unemployed persons. Any employee whose hours are involuntarily reduced to fewer than forty hours is defined as a part-time worker. In every recession or depression, the number of people who can find only part-time jobs and those who are too discouraged to look for work rises rapidly. These categories of unemployed people have risen considerably so far in the Great Recession. The BLS calculates alternative unemployment rates that include these categories and therefore go a long way toward correcting the shortcomings of the official unemployment rate. The broadest alternative measure of unemployment, called U-6, corrects for discouraged workers by counting as unemployed any person who currently wants a job, is available to work, and has looked for work in the last year. The U-6 unemployment rate also counts anyone involuntarily employed as unemployed.

Making those adjustments for May 2009, the unemployment rate soars to 16.4 percent. That was the highest rate since the BLS began calculating the U-6 rate in 1994 (for historical comparisons with earlier unemployment rates, see Bregger and Haugen 1995).

**The Misery and Waste of Unemployment**

The human misery of unemployment repeats itself with every downturn of the roller coaster economy. Unemployment even continues, if to a much lesser degree, when the economy expands. With each contraction of the economy, the social costs of this seemingly irrational economic system mount.

*Losses to Society*

Society suffers many types of losses from the contractions during business cycles. As the Great Recession has continued, thousands of factories have stood idle and millions of employees were unemployed, so society lost an enormous amount of potential output that could have been consumed. Society also lost potential production because very few new plants and very little new equipment were produced. This meant there was very little, if any, growth of productive potential for future expansion during the Great Recession. For that reason, every recession or depression lowers the long-run rate of growth. Society also has lost the new inventions that were not discovered because there was less money for research and development. Society lost because millions of people were unable to work and to create to the best of their potential. Society lost because millions of people were frustrated and unhappy, and the social atmosphere was poisoned.

### Losses to Employees

The greatest misery of the business cycle, however, is caused by the involuntary unemployment of millions of people. Every one of these individuals suffers the disruption of a useful life. Heads of families may not be able to maintain the standard of living to which their family is accustomed. Unemployed workers feel useless, believing their job loss is a personal failure. There is a measurable increase in mental and physical illness among the unemployed and their families. Increased unemployment is associated with increases in alcoholism, divorce, child abuse, crime, and even suicide. According to a grim, startling study published by the Joint Economic Committee of Congress (Brenner 1976), a sustained 1 percent increase in unemployment is associated with the following statistically significant percentage increases:

> suicide: 4.1 percent
> state mental hospital admissions: 3.4 percent
> state prison admissions: 4.0 percent
> homicide: 5.7 percent
> deaths from cirrhosis of the liver: 1.9 percent
> deaths from cardiovascular diseases: 1.9 percent

### Social Problems Caused by Unemployment

The unemployed begin to feel isolated from society and alienated from others. They feel weak, unable to change their lives, and certainly unable to change society. Rather than combining with other people to protest, they often even stop voting in elections. They do not demand to know how a political candidate intends to reduce unemployment. Many simply withdraw from any action and feel helpless. They often lapse into mental depression. As shown above, the percentage of people with mental sickness rises in every area with heavy unemployment.

Unemployment often leads to unhappy marriages, especially if a spouse is convinced that a partner's unemployment is due to that partner's own laziness or stupidity. The data also show a close relationship between the percentage of unemployed people and the percentage of couples that get divorces. Every time the marriage of a couple with children is terminated, the children are harmed. After a divorce, some children withdraw into themselves. Other children become unruly. There are many minor symptoms of the unhappiness of children of divorced parents—for example, a rise in the number of children who stutter.

Another social problem worsened by unemployment is crime. In those communities in which many young adults have no jobs, they first sit around and talk about how bad things are. Then they are easy targets for gangs to recruit them to become criminals. People who ordinarily would not stoop to crime may see it as the only option to feed their family.

Crime rises in each city in very close relationship to the amount of unemployment. How is it possible to get rid of crime? People are willing to risk a jail sentence if they need to feed themselves or their family. But as soon as jobs open up, there are thousands of unemployed who show up to compete for just a few jobs. In a recession or depression, the newspapers carry many photographs of these long lines.

These facts tell us the easiest way to reduce crime rapidly: just increase employment. People who have good jobs seldom go out to rob the corner grocery store. People who have no jobs just get more and more desperate.

## The Hunt for Clues Begins

Americans can begin to solve the mystery by recognizing the following.

First, the business cycle is not a myth but a hard fact. The economy does not follow a path of steady growth, nor does it quickly return to it from any dislocation. Rather, there is a systematic pattern of expansions and contractions. In every expansion, production across the economy increases, while it falls in every contraction.

Second, the unemployment rate falls in every expansion, but rises in every contraction. The unemployment in a contraction, whether it is a small recession or a vast depression, is involuntary. This is shown by two undeniable facts. Millions of people are fired at the same time, with no choice. And advertisements for new jobs drop to a very small number.

Third, capitalism suffers from the curse of crises and recessions or depressions at the end of every period of prosperity. The result is periods of mass unemployment. Mass unemployment leads to feelings of isolation, weakness, and hopelessness for millions of individuals. For many of these people, the end result is loss of hope and dignity, loss of a spouse, mental illness, physical illness, and, in rare cases, suicide.

In the Great Recession, those costs are being visited upon Americans more than ever before since the Great Depression.

# 2

# History of the Roller Coaster

The roller coaster economy did not always exist. Its cycles of boom and bust are found only in certain societies that have the right kind of conditions to nourish a business cycle of boom and bust. By way of introduction, it is worth mentioning a few kinds of economic structures that have existed in the world.

For over a hundred thousand years, people lived in prehistoric societies, based on hunting animals and gathering fruits and vegetables. Necessity forced everyone to work together in groups and to consume their food as a collective family group. Thus, prehistoric peoples had no exchange of goods and services in a market place, no use of money, and no private profit making.

This chapter will show that these three conditions—exchange in the market place, use of money and credit, and the making of private profit—are the necessary ingredients of the boom and bust economy, resembling a roller coaster.

The economy that preceded the modern type in Europe was called a feudal economy. At its height in the medieval period, around 1200, most people lived on farms. The feudal lord had a large estate with a farm on it. Most of the people were serfs, who were bound to the land and forced to work for the feudal lord. Both the lord's estate and the tiny farms of the serfs were self-sufficient, designed to produce just what the people living on them absolutely needed. Thus, feudalism had no permanent daily market places, little use of money, and no production for profit.

This all changed under the modern economic system called capitalism. There is a great deal of evidence that the business cycle of boom and bust is not found in any other system than capitalism (see, e.g., Sherman 2006; or Mitchell and Thorp 1926, p. 47).

**The Capitalist System**

Exactly what is meant by capitalism? One group of individuals, the capitalists, owns the means of production. The means of production, such as factories and equipment, are called capital goods. The capitalists hire other people. These employees own nothing productive but their power to labor. The capitalists own the product of the employees' labor. The capitalists sell the product in the marketplace for money. The capitalists will produce only so long as they expect to make a profit in the market above and beyond all their expenses.

The capitalist system is what creates the possibility of a roller coaster cycle of boom and bust with episodes of massive unemployment. Previous economic systems, such as slavery and feudalism, did have unemployment at times, but only rarely and usually as a result of some natural catastrophe such as a flood or an epidemic—an external shock. Only modern capitalism shows a systematic business cycle with periods of mass unemployment caused by declining profit and a lack of demand.

This chapter offers a close look at how capitalist institutional arrangements, not present in previous systems, give rise to the present roller coaster, called the business cycle.

**Production for the Market**

In the United States, the transformation to a market economy took place in the nineteenth century. The United States in 1800 was mostly a land of self-sufficient farms. When most economic units are self-sufficient, there is no market. Since the farmers did not bring most of their produce to market, there could be no problem of lack of demand for their goods in the market. Since demand was not a problem, there could be no recession nor any unemployment.

By 1900, the country had become a land of factories that had to sell their goods on the market in order to continue production. If millions of consumers did not buy enough automobiles, automobile workers lost their jobs. Thus, the transition to a market economy was one condition for a business cycle that would threaten most economic units.

In these capitalist economies beginning to take hold in Europe and the United States, where privately produced goods and services were sold in the market, the market became the chief means of generating income. Shop owners, factory owners, factory workers, those workers in their home all depended on the sale of the product of their labor to obtain an income. Whether products were sold depended on the purchasing decisions of millions of people. The buyers of products included fellow workers, factory owners, the land-owning

15

aristocracy, shopkeepers, and professionals. The mass of these purchasing decisions made up the total, or aggregate, demand or spending decision on the market economy.

In previous economic systems, the self-sufficient economic unit, the farmer or crafts person, produced a trickle of handmade items for known customers. When an economic unit consumed almost all that it produced, supply necessarily matched demand. Under capitalism, however, all the goods and services must be sold in the market if production is to continue. Production for the market, thus, is the first precondition for a business cycle.

## Money

With the coming of capitalism in Western Europe and the United States, another drastic change in economic institutions was the regular use of money in market transactions. Money was a necessary ingredient in the stew that led to the emergence of a business cycle of boom and bust.

The monetary system took the place of the barter system used in medieval feudal Europe and in the early Western United States. In the barter system, one good is exchanged for another good. Thus, a farmer brings pigs to the market and exchanges them for a cow.

Money replaced the barter system because money is much more convenient to use. But the widespread reliance on money allows economies to suffer from a lack of spending. Not enough aggregate demand expressed in money may lead to a recession or depression.

To explain why money is so helpful to the economy (when it works well), this chapter will look at the different functions of money in the modern economy. Economists usually identify four different functions of money.

The first function of money is that it serves as a general standard of value. In other words, money is a measuring stick for everything else. All contracts are drawn up in monetary terms, with so much money to be paid for a certain product at a certain time. Therefore, a coat or a table is worth so much money.

A second function of money is that it acts as the medium of exchange. In other words, money is the intermediary between one good and another. In the monetary economy, a commodity is exchanged for money. The money may then be exchanged for another commodity. But of course, a person who sells something for money may decide not to spend that money. If enough people decide not to spend their money for the goods on the market, then down the economy goes into a recession.

A third function of money is to provide a store of value. In other words, when money is received as an income, it need not be spent immediately. Instead, it can be stored away or hoarded until the possessor chooses to spend it. In the modern world, money is deposited in a bank account, where it may remain a long time.

The last function of money is that it measures payments on loans deferred to a future time. A borrower who gets a loan does not have to pay it back right now, but does have to pay a certain sum of money at some particular time. In a credit economy, this function of measuring future payments on debts becomes far more important than paper money paid immediately. It opens the way to many more problems when people cannot pay back their loans.

**The Abuses of Money**

The problem in a capitalist economy is not a lack of money in the economy as a whole. There are people who wish to buy, but may have no money. Yet there are also people who have money but may not wish to spend it at present.

If people do not spend money income for consumer goods or services, they may still invest that money in equipment and buildings. If they do not spend their money income for consumption or for investment, then they leave it idle. Idle money reduces spending in the economy. Nonspending can slow or stop the flow of money through the economy at any point. When the flow of money slows or stops, so too does the flow of products through the economy, since products are only produced to be sold for money.

As the economy turns down in a recession, many people lose jobs and no longer have money to purchase even necessities. Without money to spend, these potential consumers are unable to buy products, which pile up in warehouses. This excess supply gets larger and larger as the economy slows. Many potential consumers in need go without because they do not have the money to buy these products.

Even those who still have an income have money problems in a recession. Where can they put their money that is safe? The only safe place is in a bank account because the government now insures money deposits up to $250,000. But bank deposits in a recession provide a tiny income. The stock market makes people think about getting rich, but in a recession, their money is buried in an avalanche of red ink.

The use of credit intensifies money problems. If Brown owes Smith, and Smith owes Johnson, and Johnson owes Martin, a break anywhere along this chain of credit circulation may be disastrous for all the later parties in the chain. If one creditor in the chain is a bank, and then that bank goes bankrupt, its fall will hurt all its depositors. When the chain of credit breaks or circulation slows way down, then this break or hesitation in one sector can harm the whole economy.

The financial panic of 2008 offers a vivid example of the disastrous effects of a break in the chain of credit. The chain broke when many house mortgage loans could not be paid. Many banks were unwilling to lend money, even to other banks, because they were unable to determine if borrowers would be able to repay their loans. In fact, many banks, saddled with bad mortgage debt, could no longer repay the money they had borrowed from other banks. With loans not available, spending of all kinds dried up. Consumers could not get loans to purchase cars. Businesses could not get loans to meet their payroll. Many products went unsold, employees lost their jobs, production plummeted, and the economy spiraled downward.

Relying on money and credit institutions makes an economy susceptible to the booms and busts of the business cycle. Does this mean that money and credit institutions are the only reason for the business cycle? No. Actually, money and credit existed in ancient Rome and in the sixteenth to eighteenth centuries in Western Europe. Yet the financial disturbances of those times were not the same as the modern type of business cycle. Financial panics cannot stop the whole economy from functioning if most of the economy is self-sufficient agricultural units and estates. Financial crises can stop the whole economy only when industry becomes dominant and relies on credit.

For example, in the late eighteenth century, a financial crisis resulted from the monetary disturbances caused by the American Revolutionary War. The new U.S. government had no way to impose taxes, so they mostly financed the war by printing new money, which resulted in galloping inflation. This panic, however, was unlike the modern business cycle. These early financial panics originated in causes external to the economy, such as wars, whereas present crises originate within the system itself.

Moreover, such early monetary panics resulted in only limited depressions in a few sectors for brief and random periods. On the contrary, the modern business cycle engulfs the broad economy for several months or years. The first truly general industrial depression appeared in 1793 in England, the first country where industry played a leading role.

In brief, before capitalism many economies extensively used money and credit with only temporary and externally caused financial panics. Conversely, in the nineteenth, twentieth, and twenty-first centuries, many recessions did not produce financial panics. This history suggests that the regular use of money and credit is a necessary prerequisite of the business cycle but not a sufficient explanation of business cycles.

**Production for Private Profit**

Production for the market and regular use of money must both be present if there is to be a roller coaster economy with business cycles. But one more capitalist institution is necessary before a business recession or depression can occur. That necessary condition is production for private profit within a system of private ownership of production facilities.

As an example of economic activity in which private profit plays no role, consider the behavior of government agencies, such as the U.S. Post Office or the unified school system of Los Angeles. Government agencies in the United States use money and use the market to buy and sell goods and services. But the agencies do not decide whether to expand or contract their services according to expected private profit.

Of course, private lobbyists constantly pressure these agencies. But suppose there were no business lobbyists and no business influence. Then government spending would be determined solely by voters according to the voters' view of human needs. Therefore, an economy run democratically by the public would not be subject to business cycles of the kind found in U.S. capitalism.

Business cycles of boom and bust are found only in countries in which the economy is primarily run by private business motivated by profit. In an economy based on private ownership of individual competing businesses, the sum of decisions to produce may not equal the sum of decisions by other individuals and businesses to buy what is produced. As a result, the sum of consumption and investment spending across the economy may not be enough to buy the entire output of the economy at present prices. No one plans the behavior of a whole private, capitalist economy. Every firm makes its own decisions based on the expectation of making a profit.

Businesses live and die for profit. Profit is just their revenue from sales less their costs of doing business. If sales at present prices drop below costs, then there is a loss. If there is significant loss, then production must be decreased and employees fired. This is how a recession begins. Only when the outlook is for profit will the firm hire employees and produce goods and services. Only then will the economy recover.

## Summary of Three Conditions

Modern business cycles did not exist in precapitalist or noncapitalist economies. Under capitalism, three conditions come into existence which, taken together, allow the economy to go up and down like a roller coaster. One condition is the use of the market as the main determinant of what is produced and what is not. Second, the existence of money means that goods and services may be produced for the present, but the money may be put away and not spent in the near future. Use of credit makes the economy even more vulnerable.

A third condition for business cycles is the predominant reliance on private profit to decide when to produce or cut back production. When these three conditions are present, an economy invariably exhibits a roller coaster of business activity that moves from expansion to recession or depression and eventual recovery.

The historical record shows that previous economies, such as the feudal economy of medieval Europe, were not subject to business cycles with large contractions due to lack of demand in the market. All capitalist economies do rely on exchange in a market economy, use of money and credit, and production for profit. Therefore, capitalist economies are roller coaster economies with an inherent possibility of a business cycle. Part III examines the actual events, based on these capitalist institutions, which always lead to boom and bust.

## Spread of Business Cycles

Precapitalist societies were subject to war and to natural disasters such as floods and droughts. Precapitalist economies, however, never rise and fall because there is not enough spending to buy all the goods they produce. The signs of the modern cycle of boom and bust arise in each economy only as capitalism begins to dominate the production system.

The modern business cycle began in England in 1793, when England was becoming the first fully developed capitalist economy. As they became capitalist economies, the business cycle spread to France in 1847 and to Germany in 1857. In the period from 1888 to 1891, as capitalism and its colonies spread further, so also did the business cycle spread further to Russia, Argentina, Brazil, Canada, South Africa, Australia, India, Japan, and China. After 1890, the business cycle assumed a truly international character with regard to all large, cyclical downturns and large, cyclical upturns. (The history of U.S. business cycles is examined below.)

The less developed countries in the early nineteenth century were mainly agricultural and did not have primarily capitalist institutions. Therefore, these countries, such as China, India, and the countries of Africa, produced no business cycle of their own. As each of these countries became a colony of the more advanced capitalist countries, however, it also joined the international business cycle. As later chapters will show, the colonies became entrapped in the international business cycles because the colonizers controlled much of their trade, investment, and finance.

## The U.S. Roller Coaster

From 1800 to the American Civil War in 1860, the British business cycle led the American business cycle by a nose. Great Britain supplied most of the manufactured goods to America, while America shipped much food and raw materials to Britain. So a rise or decline in British business affected the smaller American economy.

From the Civil War to World War I in 1914, the British roller coaster and the American roller coaster interacted more or less as equals. In this period, the U.S. economy expanded rapidly, but did suffer several depressions. The worst was the depression of the 1890s, when the unemployment rate rose to 18 percent and stayed at double-digit levels for six years.

In the 1920s, the U.S. economy grew rapidly, but also endured three short recessions. Then the Great Depression struck, lasting a full decade from 1929 to 1939. Economies across the globe collapsed during the 1930s. From 1929 to 1932, gross domestic product, the broadest measure of national output, dropped 28 percent in the United States, 16 percent in Germany, 8 percent in Japan, and 6 percent in Britain (Aldcroft 1993, p. 64).

The official unemployment rate in the United States reached 25 percent, but the actual unemployment rate was yet higher. Businesses went bankrupt, banks foreclosed on mortgages, pushing homeowners out of their houses, wages fell, and prices dropped. The decrease in output in every sector of the economy was enormous. The output of the economy remained depressed for most of the ten years. Because people had little or no money to spend, there was little demand for what was produced. Even as people went hungry, farmers, at the behest of government officials, burned mounds of potatoes and tomatoes because no one could pay for them.

In 1941, World War II saved the United States from the Great Depression. The U.S. government bought 40 percent of the gross domestic product for war purposes at the height of the war effort. This massive government spending provided plenty of demand and jobs. The war pushed the official unemployment rate to 1 percent. By 1943, there was a shortage of labor because unlimited numbers of people were needed for the army and for production of war supplies.

Since the war, the U.S. economy has grown rapidly for long periods, punctuated by relatively mild and short recessions. These recessions meant misery to millions of people, but never threatened the economy with a long depression. All in all, from 1800 to the present, there have been thirty-six recessions or depressions, causing economic stagnation and human harm.

This book examines closely the five most recent U.S. business cycles. These five cycles begin with the expansion of 1970 and continue through the recession of 2001. The book shows how people have fared over that period. The book then turns to the Bush expansion of 2001 to 2007 and the Great Recession that followed it, including the crisis of 2008.

### The Expansion, 2001 to 2007

Some features of the expansion of the Bush years, 2001 to 2007, are worth noting here, with the chapters that cover them in parentheses:

- The economy grew more slowly than in the previous five expansions (Chapter 3).
- Wages and salaries grew slower than in the last five cycles, but corporate profit grew with amazing speed (Chapter 4).
- Jobs declined in the first two years of the expansion, then grew slowly (Chapter 3).
- Credit grew and grew far faster than in most previous expansions (Chapter 8).
- Housing grew rapidly, but with mortgages that many people had no chance of paying (Chapter 6).

Other features will have to wait until their foundations are examined.

### The Great Recession, 2007 to 2009

By the time the recession began in the fourth quarter of 2007, housing prices had been declining for more than a year (Chapter 6). Corporate profit was becoming stagnant (Chapter 7). The risky mortgages were held by financial companies, so when the mortgages were foreclosed, it caused a financial panic (Chapters 6 and 8).

Other factors played more important roles than housing in causing the recession, but housing certainly was one of the chief actors starting it. Discussion of this and other issues must be postponed till the logical steps are built leading to these conclusions.

All cyclical downturns have most features in common, but also some unique features. In 2007, before the beginning of the Great Recession in December, one could see the usual signals of economic distress. Later chapters will show that most forms of aggregate revenue, such as all consumer spending, had slowed their rate of growth (the word "aggregate" means in the whole economy). Most parts of aggregate cost, such as oil prices and interest rates, were rising rapidly. Profit comes from revenue minus cost. So aggregate profit slowed down and then fell. In addition, however, in this particular expansion, housing prices had been falling since 2006, while banks were issuing an amazing flood of dangerous-looking loans—usually signs of a recession turning into a depression.

The contraction from 2007 to 2009 is called the Great Recession for obvious

22

reasons. By 2009, it was already the longest and most severe contraction since the Great Depression of the 1930s. The financial crisis, the housing bust, and a downturn in the global economy combined to create a level of economic distress unprecedented since the 1930s. In 2008 alone the U.S. economy lost 2.6 million jobs. Not since the Great Depression has the economy lost jobs every month of a year as it did in 2008.

The signs of economic distress were not confined to the labor market. In the fall of 2008, consumer spending registered a large decline, unlike the tiny decline in the 2001 recession. As household incomes declined, employees lost jobs, and consumers cut back on spending. Worried consumers reduced their household debt for the first time since the Great Depression. As consumers scrimped, retail sales plummeted. Major retailers, even eBay, fired employees while others, such as Circuit City, went out of business. Prices fell significantly in 2008, the first annual drop since 1949. All the major capitalist economies went into recession in 2008 and got worse in 2009.

The crisis of 2008 and the following recession illustrate dramatically the main point of this chapter. Capitalist economies are vulnerable to a cycle of expansion and recession or even severe recession. The details of the cyclical process are discussed in the rest of this book.

**Structural Changes Leading to a Severe Contraction**

Why was the expansion of 2001 to 2007 a weak one? Why was the contraction that followed severe? To answer these questions, this section looks at the most vital structural changes that have occurred in the economy and how these have changed the business cycle.

From the early 1970s to the present, the gap between total employee income and total business profits has increased from cycle to cycle. This gap reflects the decline of manufacturing, which paid high wages. It also reflects the long-run decline of union strength. It also reflects that economic growth is slower and creates fewer jobs than in the past. These changes in the economic structure, as well as their effect in making the end of the Bush expansion more drastic, are examined fully in Chapter 4.

These changes in the structure of the labor market, and the sluggish wage and salary incomes that resulted, have limited consumer spending. Only by an ever-rising amount of credit could people keep up their usual standard of living. The continuous rise in credit changed the structure of finance and made it very fragile. These changes and their effect on the business cycle are spelled out in Chapter 8.

Thus, the focus of this book is the business cycle and its ups and downs that look like a roller coaster. But the roller coaster cannot be explained without casting a strong light on the weakening structure of the pylons on which it stands.

**Three Major Themes of This Book**

One major theme of this book is the hunt for clues to the mystery of how an expansion becomes a recession or a Great Recession. The chapters explain how the behavior of various economic variables is molded by the basic structure of the capitalist economic system.

A second major theme is how the change of economic structure led to such a severe crisis in 2008. These structural changes have been reflected in ever-rising levels of credit along with stagnant wages and salaries, after adjustment for inflation.

The final theme is that the cycles and the structure do not move by some natural law. Rather, they reflect the interests of different groups. Any human structure can be changed by a policy decision if the movement behind it is strong enough. For example, in the last forty years, bankers fought to end financial regulation, they won, and that was one cause of the depth of the crisis of 2008. In 2008, the Great Recession and the desire for change put President Barack Obama into power. Chapter 12 discusses President Obama's reforms and what is needed to end cycles and crises.

**Clues to Remember**

This chapter found that capitalism includes three important features. First, all goods and services are sold in the marketplace. Second, the goods and services are exchanged for money in the marketplace. Third, all production is conducted with the aim of making a profit. These three features are necessary conditions for the business cycle to exist. For this reason, business cycles do not exist under other economic institutions, but only under capitalist economic institutions.

**Appendix: Is the Economy Self-Regulating? Some Strange Ideas Among Economists**

All conventional economists were shocked in 1929 that a depression, including a financial crisis, could occur in a capitalist economy because they believed that the economy is self-regulating. Economists were similarly shocked in 2008 due to the severe recession and financial crisis. But the following chapters will show that a very clear pattern repeats itself in every expansion, which always results in recession or depression. The same process leads to recession or depression, but certain additional factors determine whether a recession turns into a depression or a Great Recession.

Most economists have paid no attention to history and conclude from their theories that capitalism is inherently stable and its competitive system is self-regulating. They conclude that supply and demand always come back into equilibrium with each other. The happy equality of supply and demand automatically brings back full employment in a short time. Economists recognize that some external shock may temporarily dislocate the economy. But no government action is necessary to restore full employment. Leave it to the market.

These two views of capitalism, the stable economy versus the roller coaster economy, were struggling openly by 1800. In that year, Jean-Baptiste Say, a French economist, tried to prove that any level of aggregate output supplied to the market in the whole economy will find enough aggregate demand in the whole economy within a fairly short time. This first crude statement of the view was called Say's Law.

Since Say wrote, most economists have rejected his crude statement, replacing it by increasingly sophisticated and complex mathematical formulations. They always maintained his basic position, however, that the capitalist economy is self-regulating. It automatically returns aggregate supply and aggregate demand to equality after every shock. No government regulations are needed. No government anticyclical action is needed.

This was the dominant view among all the leading economists from about 1800 until the Great Depression in the 1930s. In that period there were only a few dissident economists who argued against that view, such as Karl Marx, Thorstein Veblen, and Wesley Mitchell. Major universities tolerated no dissension from the assumption that their capitalist economy is self-regulating and automatically returns to full employment after every outside shock. Almost all economists reached the same conservative and reassuring view of the capitalist economy.

This view that the economy always returns automatically to full employment was dealt a harsh blow by the Great Depression. Many economists first tried to deny its severity, and then developed theories to say that all economies went through such readjustments and recovered automatically.

Finally, in 1936, John Maynard Keynes, famous as an orthodox economist, wrote a very unorthodox book. He destroyed the view that full employment was automatic under capitalism. He showed how the capitalist economy could fall far below full employment and stay there a long time. He advocated a government stimulus package to get the economy out of the depression, as well as government regulations and structural changes to ensure that such a fall would never happen again.

The Great Depression so worried most economists that by the end of World War II Keynes's view became the new orthodoxy. It was dominant around the world for many years. In the 1930s, two other major economists helped formulate new views that had a great deal of influence during the period from the 1930s onward. Michael Kalecki was the first economist to publish a multi-equation model that explained the expansion and contraction in terms of profit movements, and then explained profit in terms of business revenues and business costs. (The crucial contributions of Keynes, Mitchell, and Kalecki are all explained in Sherman 1991.) The third important economist who challenged conventional wisdom was Wesley Mitchell, who showed how expansions become recessions and recessions become expansions. Mitchell's empirical approach founded the factual research into the business cycle and is discussed in the next chapter.

But economists, like most people, have short memories for unpleasant facts. By the late 1960s, the dominant Keynesian view was being challenged and replaced. The new conservatives claimed that the Great Depression could never be repeated. As Chapter 8 will show, some said that the regulations imposed on business in the 1930s, plus a watered-down version of Keynesian taxations and spending policies, would keep capitalism stable. Soon, some went further. They maintained that since capitalism is self-regulating, the regulations imposed by governments in the 1930s were no longer needed. Any government action, as advocated by Keynes, was unnecessary. To make a long story short, the old conservative economic views again became dominant by the 1970s and were still dominant when the Great Recession began in 2007. They got rid of most financial regulations and downplayed any need to study the art of stimulus.

The current economic crisis has shaken some of even the most devoted believers in the inherent stability of the self-regulating market economy. On October 23, 2008, Alan Greenspan spoke to a congressional hearing investigating the causes of the global financial crisis. Greenspan was the chair of the Federal Reserve System for twelve years, and colleagues and commentators referred to him as the "oracle" or the "maestro." For those twelve years, he fought against any attempt to regulate the financial system and led the successful fight to dismantle many of the regulations and safeguards that had been put in place after the Great Depression.

Greenspan told the House Committee on Oversight and Government Reform that the extreme financial crisis had left him in "in a state of shocked disbelief" (Towns 2008). He claimed that no one predicted this "once-in-a-century credit tsunami" because it defied the characteristics of a self-regulated capitalist economic system, operating with competition for private profit. Yet, he said, this self-regulating tendency of the economy toward equilibrium at full employment is well known to every economist. He then admitted that he had been wrong to deregulate finance to such an extreme degree because the system was not self-regulating as he had assumed. "I made a mistake," Greenspan confessed, "in presuming that the self-interests of organizations, specifically banks and others, were such that they were best capable of protecting their own shareholders" (see the details of the testimony in Scannell and Reddy 2008, p. 1).

This book will clarify the problem of why the capitalist economy continues to have severe recessions and financial crises.

**Poetic Comment**
*By Paul Sherman*

The rate of profit, it ebbs and it flows,
On which we depend for home, food, and clothes.
When people are employed they spend and demand
From which follows investment as a corporate plan.

Production continues and grows without bound,
Touches the sky, then turns back around.
Mitchell measures the pattern and counts each price tag.
We'll soon see it's just with a two-quarter time lag.

All sorts of institutions in a Veblenesque sense
From whom give us salary and to whom we pay rents
Have evolved from the feudal ball and chains,
Each producing and consuming often, says Keynes.

From Adam Smith we know the wealth of a nation
And poverty and depression from capitalism's creation.
Getting people equal work that is fair
Is Marx's idea of labor without profit share.

# 3

# How Unstable Is the American Economy?

This chapter looks at the long run growth of the U.S. economy since World War II. Then it defines the business cycle more carefully, shows the easiest way to measure it, and then constructs a picture of it with the help of graphs on some broad measures of employment and output. The broadest measure of output is the gross domestic product, always called GDP by economists. The GDP is the name for all of the goods and services produced by the U.S. economy. If you go to a party and whisper GDP to enough people, they will think you are an expert.

## Structural Change: The Golden Age of GDP Growth

During the golden age of American capitalism, the first two decades after World War II, the U.S. economy grew rapidly. The growth lifted employee incomes and alleviated poverty. American banks and corporations loaned money to foreign banks and corporations. The United States was the largest creditor country in the world. The United States exported far more than it imported, so money flowed into the economy. This excess of exports over imports is called a favorable balance of trade or a trade surplus. The U.S. economy produced more than the rest of the world put together for a while, while also trading more than the rest of the world put together.

With its dominant position in the world economy, the U.S. economy grew an average of 4.4 percent a year from 1950 to 1969 (Table 3.1). America had strong trade unions and expanding government programs to protect employees. There were also programs to fight poverty, which spread the benefits of economic growth to most Americans.

## Structural Change: Lower Growth of GDP

The U.S. economy grew rapidly in the 1950s and 1960s, but in the next three decades, 1970 to 2000, the U.S. economy grew more slowly. Not

Table 3.1

**Gross Domestic Product, Real U.S. Dollars, Annual Rate
of Growth per Decade**

| Decade | Average GDP growth rate (in percent) |
|---|---|
| 1950–1959 | 4.38 |
| 1960–1969 | 4.40 |
| 1970–1979 | 3.39 |
| 1980–1989 | 3.13 |
| 1990–1999 | 3.27 |

*Source:* Calculated from Bureau of Economic Analysis data files. Table 1.2.1: Percentage Change From Preceding Period in Real Gross Domestic Product by Major Type of Product. Seasonally adjusted at annual rates (see www.bea.gov).

only did GDP grow more slowly, but many other developments also weakened the U.S. economy. Production in other countries rose faster than U.S. production. Therefore, the U.S. share of world production dropped. The American economy went from being the largest creditor to being the largest debtor. America changed from having the largest trade surplus to having the largest trade deficit. The percentage of workers in trade unions steadily declined.

Inequality between poor and rich Americans had declined in the period from 1950 to 1970. In the period from 1970 to the present, inequality between rich and poor rose continuously in every decade.

Over this long period, GDP growth slowed considerably from the 4.4 percent a year in the 1950–1969 period. It was only 3.4 percent a year in the 1970–2000 period. This decline may be seen very clearly in Figure 3.1.

During this period of slower growth, unions and employees lost ground in the struggle over who gets what out of national income. This shift in income distribution happened partly because social spending programs and government protections were gutted. As a result, what economic growth there was did less to raise average employee incomes and alleviate poverty than economic growth of the 1950s and 1960s had.

**Defining a Business Cycle**

Wesley Mitchell invented the simplest method to paint a picture of the business cycle and he founded the National Bureau of Economic Research, which tracks the cycle (see Burns and Mitchell 1946; for a discussion of Mitchell's work, see Sherman 2001). Mitchell was the greatest researcher into the facts

Figure 3.1  **Gross Domestic Product by Decade, 1950–1999**

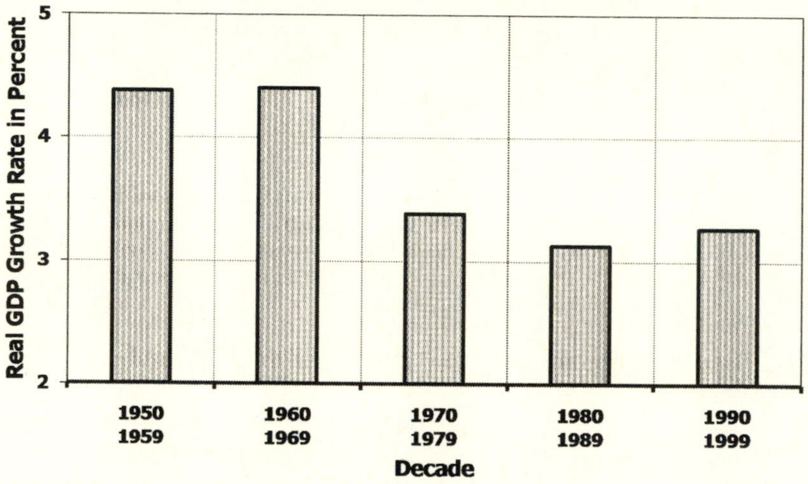

*Source:* Bureau of Economic Analysis, Department of Commerce (www.bea.gov).
*Note:* Gross domestic product. Percent change, quarter to quarter, 1950 to 1999 in billions of chained 2000 dollars. (Chained 2000 dollars means that all of the series is corrected for inflation with a base of the year 2000.) Seasonally adjusted quarterly data aggregated to decade data, at annual rates.

of the business cycle in the twentieth century and, along with his coauthor Burns, defined it this way:

> Business cycles are a type of fluctuation found in the aggregate economic activity of nations that organize their work mainly in business enterprises; a cycle consists of expansions occurring at about the same time in many economic activities, followed by similarly general recessions, contractions, and revivals, which merge into the expansion phase of the next cycle; this sequence of changes is recurrent but not periodic. In duration business cycles vary from more than one year to ten or twelve years. (Burns and Mitchell 1946, p. 3)

It is worth examining each of the points in Mitchell's definition. First, as shown in the last chapter, business cycles are found in capitalist economies, not in other systems. Second, the business cycle is not limited to a single industry, but is economy-wide. Third, one cycle is similar in some ways to another. All cycles are marked by similar sequences of events. Fourth, cycles differ, however, in many ways, including how long they last and how deep the recession goes.

Not everyone is convinced that the business cycle is a real economic phenomenon. In fact, during every economic boom a number of economic observers, including economists, business writers, politicians and others, doubt the existence of the business cycle or claim that it is a thing of the past. The number of economists and politicians doubting the existence of the business cycle rises almost with each year of sustained economic growth. As the first chapter disclosed, many such claims of the disappearance of all depressions were made in 1929 just before the stock market crash. The sheer number of such claims again reached a crescendo in 2000 at the end of a record breaking ten years of economic growth.

The Great Recession and the financial crisis of 2008 convinced most people that the business cycle still exists. For instance, following the financial collapse in September 2008, Stephen Adler, the editor-in-chief of *Business Week*, a leading U.S. business magazine, reminded his readers that,

> the business cycle is real. In the '90s, the smartest people were telling us that the Internet revolution had vanquished the business cycle by sending productivity on a perpetual upward climb. Economic laws no longer applied. And then the bubble burst. In the '00s, the smartest people were telling us that Wall Street had vanquished the business cycle by gaining mastery over risk. No mortgage was too absurd, no leverage too great, no structured product too reckless when risk-spreading models were brilliantly engineered. Common sense laws no longer applied. And then the bubble burst, again. (2008)

Adler is right. The business cycle is real and continues to shape the economy.

## Dating a Business Cycle

The National Bureau of Economic Research (NBER), a private research organization founded by Mitchell, is designated by the Commerce Department as the nation's arbiter of the business cycle. The NBER determines the dates of the business cycles in the U.S. economy.

Following Mitchell's definition, the NBER has identified thirty-two complete business cycles in which the U.S. economy rose and then declined in the years from 1854 to 2007. Nine cycles have occurred since World War II. This book concentrates on the period from 1970 to the present. Before 1970, the United States had many ties to the global economy, but the country became far more integrated into the global economy in the early 1970s. The exact dates and duration of the five complete business cycles from 1970 to 2001, and the expansion of 2001 to 2007 are given in Table 3.2.

Table 3.2 reports the dates of business cycle troughs and peaks, revealing the length of each cycle and of its expansions and contractions. The table reports these dates and lengths in quarters. There are three months in a quarter. Quarters are used because months are too short and years too long for

Table 3.2

**Troughs and Peaks of the Business Cycle**

| Initial trough | Peak | Final trough |
|---|---|---|
| 1970.4 | 1973.4 | 1975.1 |
| 1975.1 | 1980.1 | 1980.3 |
| 1980.3 | 1981.3 | 1982.4 |
| 1982.4 | 1990.3 | 1991.2 |
| 1991.2 | 2001.1 | 2001.4 |
| 2001.4 | 2007.4 | ? |

*Source:* National Bureau of Economic Research (www.nber.org).
*Note:* Initial Trough, Peak, and Final Trough are reference dates for U.S. Business Cycle Expansions and Contractions. Initial Trough is the same as the Final Trough of the previous cycle.

convenient division of the cycle. The average cycle from 1970 to 2001 was about five years long. But these five cycles ranged in length from a little over two years to nearly eleven years.

**The GDP Over the Cycle**

The GDP measures the dollar value of U.S.-produced goods and services. As the largest variable that measures economic output, GDP provides the best single indicator of the aggregate business activity. In addition, GDP typically reaches its own peak at the peak of the business cycle. Furthermore, GDP reaches a trough at both the initial trough and the final trough of the business cycle. This is shown in Figure 3.2.

Figure 3.2 shows the usual behavior of GDP, corrected for inflation (which economists call "real" GDP), over a typical business cycle. This figure shows the classic pattern of the business cycle. Output measured by real GDP rises in the economic expansion and falls in the economic contraction. So does almost every part of it, from the production of consumer durables, such as automobiles, to the provision of services at beauty parlors and barbershops. While each part of the economy rises and falls at different speeds, GDP shows the average rise and fall of all goods and services.

In Figure 3.2, there are nine stages depicted along the bottom axis. Stage 1 represents the first quarter of the cycle, at its initial trough or bottom. Stages 2, 3, and 4 divide the rest of the expansion into three equal pieces.

Stage 5 is at the peak of the cycle and is just one-quarter in length. After the peak, the recession is divided into three equal pieces, called stages 6, 7, and 8. The final trough is called stage 9 and is one-quarter long.

On the left side of the figure is the label "Percent of cycle average." The average is the sum of all the values over the cycle, divided by the number of

Figure 3.2 **Gross Domestic Product by Cycle, 1970–2001**

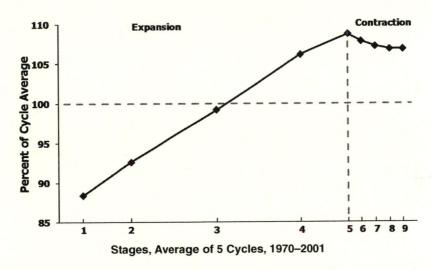

**Stages, Average of 5 Cycles, 1970–2001**

*Source:* Bureau of Economic Analysis, U.S. Department of Commerce (www.bea.gov).
   *Note:* Real gross domestic product. Average of five cycles, 1970.4 to 2001.4, in billions
of chained 2000 dollars. Quarterly, seasonally adjusted.

quarters. All the points on the graph are percentages of the average. As an example, if the GDP goes 5 percent above the average in some stage, it will be at 105 on the graph. If the GDP goes 5 percent under its average, it will be at 95 percent, or 95 on the graph.

   Since the graph depicts percentages, it can be used to compare the rise and fall of tons of steel with toothbrushes or GDP. This method can also easily average a variable over several cycles. In Figure 3.2 the data represent the average percentages of GDP over five cycles. This kind of graph is very simple, but very useful, so it is used in all cycle graphs in the book. Readers who want the technical details can refer to the spreadsheet program at www. mesharpe-student.com.

**Unemployment Over the Business Cycle**

The most usual indicator of the use of available employees is the unemployment rate. Of course, the amount of employment rises in expansions and declines in contractions. Therefore, as shown in detail in Chapter 1, the unemployment rate falls in every expansion and rises in every contraction. This behavior is pictured at each point in the business cycle in the usual cycle graph in Figure 3.3.

Figure 3.3 **Unemployment Rate by Cycle, 1970–2001**

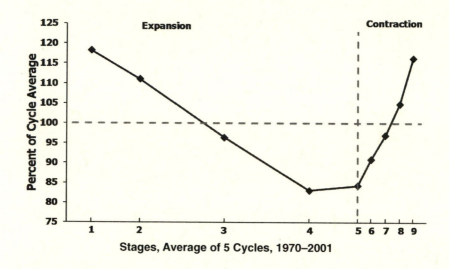

**Stages, Average of 5 Cycles, 1970–2001**

*Source:* Bureau of Labor Statistics, U.S Department of Labor (www.bls.gov).
   *Note:* Unemployment rate is the ratio of all unemployed workers to all members of the
civilian labor force, as a percentage. Average of five cycles, 1970.4 to 2001.4. Quarterly,
seasonally adjusted.

Figure 3.3 shows the normal behavior of unemployment for the five booms
and recessions from 1970 to 2001. The unemployment rate falls in expansions
because an expanding economy needs more employees. The unemployment
rate rises in contractions because a shrinking economy needs fewer employees.
This rise and fall of unemployment is one of the clearest facts of the business
cycle. This systemic unemployment should never be forgotten when looking
at any individual unemployed person, who is the victim of an unpleasant
economic system.

## GDP in the Bush Expansion, 2001 to 2007

This chapter has discussed the normal behavior of GDP and unemployment
in the five cycles from 1970 to 2001. Now it turns to the new situation that
developed under President George W. Bush, when an unusually weak expansion was followed by a crisis and Great Recession. Figure 3.4 shows what
happened to GDP each year of the Bush expansion.
   The U.S. economy grew more slowly in the expansion of 2001 to 2007 than
in any of the earlier recessions since World War II. GDP grew at an anemic
rate of 2.49 percent a year in that expansion. It is important to understand

Figure 3.4  **Gross Domestic Product by Year, 2001–2007**

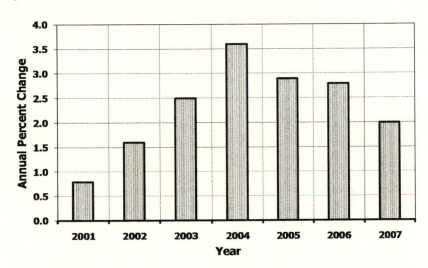

*Source:* Bureau of Economic Analysis, U.S. Department of Commerce (www.bea.gov).
   *Note:* Real gross domestic product. Percent change, year-to-year, 2001 to 2007, in billions of chained 2000 dollars. Annual data.

that what made most Americans unhappy with the expansion under President Bush was that most of the income generated by an increased GDP went to the wealthy and much less went to the middle class and the poor, as shown in the next chapter.

Since most other things in the economy depend to some extent on the GDP, it is worth taking a glance at how GDP actually behaved year by year. Figure 3.4 shows with unusual clarity that the rate of growth of GDP each year rose to the middle of the expansion, and then started slowing down. In other words, in the last half of the expansion, the GDP grew, but it grew slower and slower. This is an important feature of almost every cycle, but it is clearer than usual in the 2001 to 2007 expansion.

Why did the GDP growth rate decline? Later chapters of this book will show that the growth rate of consumption and the growth rate of investment followed the same pattern. In examining consumption and investment, the reader will have to follow the clues—like Sherlock Holmes—to see why the slowing growth rate finally declined in the last half of the expansion.

**Unemployment in the Bush Expansion, 2001 to 2007**

Have things changed in the latest expansion and contraction? Yes and no. The basic cyclical rise and fall of employment has been repeated. But some

35

Figure 3.5 **Unemployment Rate by Year, 2001–2007**

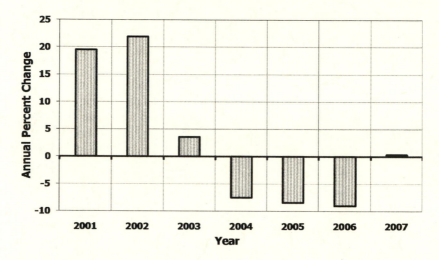

*Source:* Bureau of Labor Statistics, U.S. Department of Labor (www.bls.gov).
*Note:* Unemployment rate is the ratio of all unemployed workers to all members of the civilian labor force. Percent change, year-to-year, 2001.1 to 2007.4, seasonally adjusted quarterly data aggregated to annual data.

trends of the last couple of recessions became far more pronounced in the Bush expansion and the Great Recession. Incidentally, saying "2001 to 2007" every time is repetitive, so except when it is important to spell it out to avoid confusion, this expansion will be called the "2001 expansion" or the "Bush expansion."

In both the expansion of the 1980s and that of the 1990s, employment was slow to recover from the previous recession, but this trend was emphasized dramatically in the expansion from 2001 to 2007. The number of jobs actually continued to decline in the first two years of the expansion, an unprecedented event. Moreover, the number of jobs did not recover to the prerecession peak until 2005, about four years into the recovery. The time it took to recover to the former job level was about twice as long as in the average of the previous five cycles.

The behavior of the GDP and unemployment in the Bush expansion may be seen in Figure 3.5.

The previous five expansions had added over 2.5 percent new jobs a year to the labor force. The 2001 expansion, however, added less than 1 percent of new jobs a year. Why was this expansion so jobless by comparison to earlier ones? Fewer jobs were needed because of the lower economic growth.

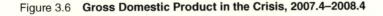

Figure 3.6   **Gross Domestic Product in the Crisis, 2007.4–2008.4**

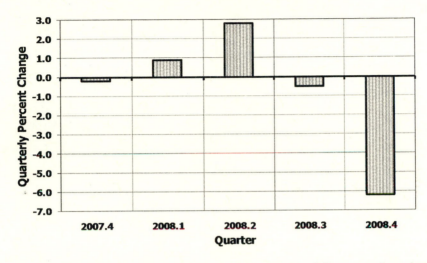

*Source:* Bureau of Economic Analysis, U.S. Department of Commerce (www.bea.
gov).
   *Note:* Real gross domestic product. Percent change, quarter-to-quarter, 2007.4 to 2008.4,
in billions of chained 2000 dollars. Seasonally adjusted quarterly data, at annual rates.

Furthermore, global competition led firms to do everything possible to use
new technology that would replace employees with machines. Moreover, with
increased global competition, American firms exported jobs to other countries
with lower wages. For example, many American corporations hired computer
savvy employees in India.

**GDP in the Great Recession, 2007 Through 2009**

While the Bush expansion of 2001 left millions of disappointed employees
with poor-paying jobs or no jobs at all, the Great Recession, beginning in late
2007, was much worse. It was a major factor in the defeat of the Republican
Party in the 2008 presidential campaign. How did GDP behave in the Great
Recession and during the financial crisis of 2008? This question is answered
pictorially in Figure 3.6.
   The Great Recession began in the last quarter of 2007, but became much
worse in 2008. There was a slight decline of GDP at the peak in the fourth
quarter of 2007. But there was still a little growth in the first half of 2008.
Then there was a tiny decline of in the third quarter of 2008. In the last quarter
of 2008, GDP declined at an annual rate of 6.3 percent. This decline was a

Figure 3.7 **Unemployment Rate in the Crisis, 2007.4–2008.4**

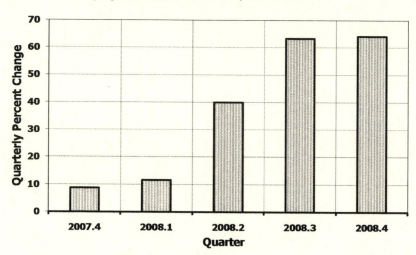

*Source:* Bureau of Labor Statistics, U.S. Department of Labor (www.bls.gov).

*Note:* Unemployment rate is the ratio of all unemployed workers to all members of the civilian labor force. Percent change, quarter to quarter, 2007.4 to 2008.4, seasonally adjusted quarterly data, at annual rates.

striking loss to society. It meant that the economy was engulfed in the worst downturn since the Great Depression.

**Unemployment in the Crisis of 2008**

During 2008, the number of jobs in the whole economy declined every single month. By December, more than half a million jobs were being lost each month. Newspapers reported thousands of job losses every day. A total of 2.6 million jobs were lost in 2008 alone.

Every day large firms announced that they were firing thousands of employees. The unemployed then had much less income than when they were previously employed. Therefore, they bought less goods and services than when they were at paid work. Of course, the reduction in total national demand caused corporations to fire more workers. It was a vicious downward spiral. The exact data are depicted in Figure 3.7.

According to Figure 3.7, unemployment rose during every one of the first five quarters of the Great Recession. The biggest increases were in the third and fourth quarters of 2008, when the intense financial crisis was spreading disaster all around. The number of job losses, however, continued to climb throughout the first quarter of 2009.

## Clues to Remember

From 1949 to 2001, there were nine recessions in the United States, with similar declines in most of the capitalist world. In these contractions, GDP suffered relatively mild declines. There was also a mild decline in the use of productive capacity, with more equipment and buildings idle. The unemployment rate rose in each of these recessions. But the decline in jobs ranged from 5 to 10 percent unemployment rates. This was far below the 25 percent unemployment of the Great Depression, so it was considered very mild, except by the millions of people who lost their jobs for a year or more.

The decline in GDP in the Great Recession of 2007 has been greater than in any of the last nine recessions. Unemployment appears to be growing to a higher level than in any of these recessions.

One important clue to the mystery of recessions and depressions is the fact that in every expansion, as in the 2001 expansion, the GDP rises fairly rapidly in the first half of expansion, then more and more slowly in the last half. The exact same trend is found in many other major economic variables, such as consumer spending. This clue shows that the causes of recession and depression are to be found in the underlying trends in the preceding expansion. Far more dramatic clues to the causes of the Great Recession, and all such contractions, will be given in the next chapter.

## Selected Readings

For the details of Wesley Mitchell's method, see the simple explanation in Sherman et al. 2008, Chapter 41. For a more advanced explanation and citations to Mitchell, see Sherman 1991, Chapter 2. Readers who wish to see how the business calculations for this book were done, as well as how to create their own spreadsheet and graphs, can refer to the actual spreadsheet program at www.mesharpe-student.com and click on the cover of the book to access the spreadsheet. Note that any reader who wishes to see how some economic series behaves over the cycle need only paste the series into the appropriate date on the spreadsheet at that site.

# Part II

# Diagnosing the Roller Coaster

Part II of this book gives a picture of how the economic roller coaster actually works. There is an explanation of how the Great Recession of 2007 through 2009 occurred. There is also an explanation of how structural changes in the American economy brought about a financial crisis in 2008 and 2009.

### Profit as the Incentive to Investment

The American economy expands when business invests in new buildings and new equipment. The American economy contracts when business decides not to invest anymore and not even to use all of the buildings and equipment that it has. What makes business decide whether to expand or to contract?

The bottom line for American business is profit. If business decides that a good profit is to be made in the future by expanding its facilities, it will do so. If a business decides that expansion will not result in a future profit, then it will not expand. If a business starts losing money rather than making profit, it will contract.

Never forget that this expansion or contraction directly affects human beings. When a business expands, it hires more employees. When a business contracts, it fires employees.

### What Determines Profit?

Profit results when the revenue of a business is greater than its costs. Therefore, the basic equation of American business, both for the individual business and in the aggregate of all business, is:

$$\text{Profit} = \text{Revenue} - \text{Costs.}$$

Suppose that Janet owns a hat store. This year, she sells $200,000 worth of hats. That is her revenue. But it costs money to get the hats and sell them.

She must pay money to buy the hats from a manufacturer, she must pay employees to sell the hats, she must pay taxes to the government, and she must pay interest on the capital she borrowed to go into business. Suppose these costs amount to $180,000. Then her profit is the revenue minus the costs, or $20,000 a year.

In the economy as a whole, the aggregate profit of business is the aggregate revenue minus the aggregate costs.

### Four Rivers of Revenue

The revenue comes from the sales in four groups: consumers, other businesses, government, and people and businesses from foreign countries. So we may think of aggregate revenue as these four rivers of spending:

Revenue = Consumption + Investment + Government + Exports

These four vast rivers of revenue flow to business. All other things being equal, the larger the four rivers are, the larger will be business profit. Consumer spending is studied in Chapter 5, investment in Chapter 7, government in Chapter 9, and foreign spending in Chapter 10. Long-run changes in housing are explored in Chapter 6, while credit is explored in Chapter 8.

### Five Mountains of Costs

There are many types of costs. For clarity, we shall examine only five of the most important costs of business. These costs are: wages, salaries, and benefits of employees; raw materials; imports other than raw materials; taxes; and interest payments. These are the "key costs" that rise and fall most in the boom and bust cycle that constitutes the roller coaster economy. Other costs are minor or do not fluctuate much. Therefore:

Key costs = Wages, salaries, and benefits + Raw materials + Imports other than raw materials + Taxes + Interest payments

If revenue is constant, then the higher the costs, the lower will be the business profit. Costs may therefore be conceived as high mountains to be climbed by business trying to get to their goal of profits. Wages, salaries, and benefits are studied in Chapter 4, both the way they move over the cycle and their long-run structural changes. Interest costs of borrowing are studied in Chapter 8. Government taxes are studied in Chapter 9. Imports of raw materials as well as imports of other commodities are studied in Chapter 10.

This framework will be applied to the facts of the roller coaster economy in the next seven chapters. The emphasis will be on the causes of the Great Recession and financial crisis of in the years 2007 to 2009. Chapters 4 through 10 will spell out the performance of each of the types of revenue and costs for the aggregate economy.

Part II will pull all of these revenues and costs into one narrative, after which the book will turn to policy issues.

# 4

# The Income Gap

This book has been following the clues of a mystery: why are there recessions and depressions, with booms in between?

**The Story So Far**

Chapter 1 showed how unemployment rises and falls with the business cycle of capitalism. The system is responsible, not the individual. That chapter also spelled out the terrible effects of unemployment on the individual and on society.

Chapter 2 revealed that the business cycle occurs only in capitalism and not in other types of societies. Other societies have had awful problems, but nothing that looks like the business cycle of capitalism. Chapter 2 introduced the latest crisis and depression in historical perspective.

Chapter 3 found that the GDP of the United States and the number of people employed both go up with the cycle and also go down with the cycle. It also showed that GDP growth has declined in recent cycles, especially during the Bush 2001 expansion. That chapter told how jobs recovered very slowly. The low growth of income and jobs helps to explain why the income of the average American fell so far behind the income of the elite in the 2001 to 2007 expansion.

**The Importance of the Income Gap**

Employee income is the largest single source of consumer spending, so in this respect it is very favorable to profits. But employee income is also the largest single cost of doing business, so it is unfavorable to profits in this respect. In every expansion, including the Bush expansion of 2001 to 2007, business succeeded in keeping costs low by limiting the growth of wages and salaries to a relatively small amount. But in detail, this success in limiting wages and salaries resulted in too little buying power to buy the increasing flood of consumer goods and services. Chapter 4 will examine this process in detail.

In the Bush expansion of 2001 to 2007, there was a rapidly increasing income gap between wages and salaries on the one hand and corporate profits on the other hand. The fact that this gap rose dramatically in the Bush expansion is crucial. It reduced the buying power of most Americans. This meant less ability to buy consumer goods and services, which caused that sector to slow its growth to a crawl. The income gap also meant less buying power to purchase new homes. It eventually limited construction and forced people to get very risky mortgages to finance their new homes. This was a major force underlying the financial crisis to come.

**Structural Changes in Income Distribution**

To understand the cycles in income, readers must understand the structural changes that have hit this area. In the 1950s and 1960s, the income of the average employee rose every year. Thus, middle-income employees had the money to afford a modest home and education for their children.

From 1970 to the present, however, wages and salaries (adjusted for inflation) have stagnated. The average middle-income employee no longer puts away some savings. Most people of average income now go into debt. This is a very drastic change in the economy and society. The details are given below.

**The Two Americas**

In terms of income, there are two Americas: the enormous class of employees and the tiny class of capitalists. It will be shown that most of the wealth goes to rich individuals, who own the giant corporations, while the average employee has a far smaller income based on the labor that is done by the employee.

As long as employees work for a firm, some of their product becomes profit. This institutionalized giveaway helps to explain the increasing trend toward inequality. "The increase in inequality," according to Larry Summers, the top economic adviser to President Obama, "meant that each family in the bottom 80 percent of the income distribution was effectively sending a $10,000 check, every year, to the top 1 percent of earners" (see Leonhardt 2009).

**Individual Distribution of Income**

The reader will find a lot of numbers in this section, and they are fascinating for what they reveal about wealth and poverty in the United States.

The usual way to look at income distribution in the United States is to compare the income of the poorest 20 percent of Americans with the richest 20 percent of Americans.

In 2005 the poorest 20 percent had less than 4 percent of all income. In the same year, however, the richest 20 percent had over 50 percent of all income. And the richest 1 percent, the superrich, had 21 percent of all income to themselves. Those are enormous differences.

Dry statistics do not move anyone emotionally, so people can bury their heads in the sand and ignore them. The poorest 20 percent has unhealthful and insufficient food. The poor also wear old clothes. The poor have housing with leaky roofs, drafty walls and windows, and sometimes rats. The richest 20 percent in this wealthy land has the finest food, beautiful clothing, and very pleasant homes. The poor have little recreation, while the rich can afford a wonderful array of recreation. The superrich live in opulence.

The above paragraphs portray the population in terms of the income they receive each year. But "wealth" is all that has been saved out of income during a person's lifetime. Wealth includes cars, homes, stock certificates, and anything else that can be turned into cash. Since most people are unable to save because they must use their whole income for necessities, only the rich can save large amounts and pile up wealth.

Wealth is, therefore, much more unequally owned than is income. In 2004, the top 1 percent of Americans owned 34 percent of all the wealth. When averaged out, the bottom 60 percent, including most of the middle-income group as well as the poor, has no wealth at all. That average of the wealth of the lowest 60 percent of Americans comes to zero because it includes not only the savings of those who are fairly well off, but also the debts and liabilities that everyone has.

Not only is there inequality in America, but this richest of all countries also has a large amount of outright poverty. According to the U.S. Census Bureau, the average poverty threshold for unrelated individuals in 2007 was an income of $10,787, and for a family of three with one child, the poverty-level income was $16,689. In 2007, 12.5 percent of the U.S. population lived in poverty, according to official government data. Nearly 11 percent of families lived below the poverty level.

For female-headed households, the numbers are even worse. In 2007, a little over 28 percent of female-headed households lived below the poverty threshold. Even more surprising is the number of working people who live below the poverty threshold. Just over 11 percent of people living below the poverty level worked year-round, full-time jobs.

The average hourly wage (for nonsupervisory workers) in 1972 was $19.32. In 2007, thirty-five years later, the average hourly wage had dropped to $17.88.

(These figures are in real dollars, that is, adjusted for inflation. Adjusting for inflation will always mean in this book using the appropriate price deflator supplied by the government.) As real wages declined, aggregate U.S. production actually rose by 180.7 percent over the same period.

Although ordinary production-line workers suffered in this period from stagnant real-wage rates, corporate chief executive officers (CEOs) did very well. The salaries of CEOs rose from 41 times the average wage in 1960 to 326 times the average wage in 1997 and to 411 times the average wage in 2005. The one thing that ordinary workers were able to increase was their debt. The debt of the average household rose from 29.5 percent of personal income in 1949 to 65 percent of personal income in the mid-1980s and then to 113 percent of personal income in 2007.

It is worth stressing that the members of the richest 1 percent—from millionaires to billionaires—make most of their income from property ownership, mainly from ownership of corporations. The only apparent exception is the salary of CEOs, but these enormous salaries are actually corporate profit for the most part. Corporations also often give CEOs the option to buy stock at very favorable prices.

On the other hand, the income of the bottom 90 percent comes primarily from wages and salaries. The bottom 90 percent, however, receives only negligible amounts of property income.

**Class Distribution of Income**

The division of income was examined above in terms of individuals at different levels of income. But there are also data on the aggregate amount of income by class. An economic class is any group of people with common interests. There are a number of significant classes in the United States, including employees, farmers, small business people, and capitalist owners of corporations. This section focuses on the employee class and the capitalist class, which are vital for understanding the business cycle.

The national income of the United States is defined by the Department of Commerce to mean all of the income received by anyone who receives income through any economic activity. National income may be divided into two categories: employee income and property income. Employee income is defined to mean wages, plus salaries, plus benefits of all kinds from employers. Thus, all employee income comes from some type of manual or intellectual labor. Property income derives purely from ownership of property. Property income is divided into rental, interest, and profit income. All U.S. business is divided into corporations and unincorporated businesses, such as individual proprietorships and partnerships. Total business profit comes from both the profit of corporations and the profit of unincorporated businesses.

Employees labor all the normal working day for a corporation or some other business. But under the economic system of capitalism, everything produced by employees goes to the employer-capitalist. When the goods or services are sold, the capitalist then pays the employee a certain wage or salary. After paying for wages and salaries, as well as raw materials and equipment, the capitalist keeps the rest of the revenue. That revenue is called "profit" by accountants. A capitalist is someone who puts in the capital of the enterprise. The capital is the cost of all the buildings and equipment of the enterprise.

Employees are over 90 percent of the population, but they get much less than that share of the national income. Capitalists who own significant capital are only about 1 percent of the population, but they have a very large percentage of the national income.

By definition, all U.S. national income is divided between employee income and property income, as explained above. The government data disclose that 69 percent of all national income goes to employee income. Therefore, 31 percent of all national income goes to property income in the form of rent, interest, and profits (see BEA 2005).

The remaining 31 percent of national income went to property income (rent, interest, and profit, which includes the profit from farms, small business, and corporations). On average, two and a half hours a day (or 31 percent) of all the labor of employees, from ditch diggers to engineers, goes to property income.

### The Increasing Income Gap

Over the five cycles from 1970 until 2001, the gap between employee income and the whole national income has grown rapidly. In other words, property income has increased much faster than employee income. The increasing income gap may be seen in Figure 4.1.

Figure 4.1 shows the increasing gap between national income and employee income since 1970. Much of the gap is due to the rapid rise of corporate profit. The increasing gap between all national income and employee income reflects the simple fact that wages and salaries have grown slowly, while corporate profit has grown rapidly.

There were five cyclical expansions between 1970 and 2001. In the average expansion, employee income rose by 3.6 percent a year, while corporate profit rose 4.9 percent a year. (All data here are in real terms, corrected for inflation, from the U.S. Department of Commerce 2009.)

### The Income Gap Over the Business Cycle, 1970 to 2001

Over a several decades, a large gap has opened between corporate profit and employee income. This section will examine exactly what happens to that

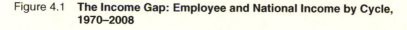

Figure 4.1 **The Income Gap: Employee and National Income by Cycle, 1970–2008**

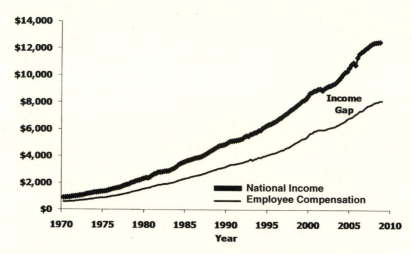

*Source:* Bureau of Economic Analysis, Department of Commerce (www.bea.gov).
*Note:* Employee income is all wages, salaries, and benefits. National income is all employee income plus all property income (rent, interest, and profits).

gap at each phase in the roller coaster economy seen in the business cycle. What does happen to the distribution of income between capitalist owners and employees in expansions and in recessions?

In every expansion, the capitalist or profit share of national income rises while the employee share of national income falls. In every expansion, profit rises rapidly, while wages and salaries move up more slowly.

The "employee share" is defined as the ratio of total employee income to the national income. The declining employee share in the average expansion is shown clearly in Figure 4.2.

Figure 4.2 shows what happened to the employee share during the average of the previous five cycles from 1970 to 2001 and in the Bush cycle of 2001 to 2008. This cycle graph line is incomplete because (at the time of this writing) nobody yet knows when the Great Recession will end.

In the average of the last five business cycles between 1970 and 2001, the employee share declined for most of the business expansion. In fact, the graph shows that the employee share declined and then remained very low for the first four stages of the business expansion, then rose slightly in the last stage of expansion.

The Bush expansion reveals the same general behavior of the employee share. The decline in expansion, however, is sharper. The decline also clearly

Figure 4.2  **Employee Share by Cycle, 1970–2001, and the Cycle of 2001–2008**

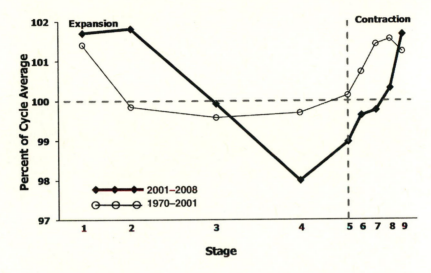

*Source:* Bureau of Economic Analysis, Department of Commerce (www.bea.gov).
*Note:* Employee share is the ratio of labor income to national income. Average of five cycles, 1970 to 2001, plus the separate cycle of 2001 to 2008 in billions of chained 2000 dollars, seasonally adjusted.

continues to stage four of the expansion. It rises again only very slightly in the brief fifth stage of the expansion. So in all of the last five cycles, the employee share declined during most of the expansion, especially in the 2001–2007 expansion. The impact of this behavior is discussed below.

On the other hand, in the average of the previous five cycles, the employee share of national income rose for most of the business recession. Only in the last stage of the average recession of the last five cycles did the employee share begin to drop once more.

In the Great Recession through 2008, there was a rapid rise of the employee share. To avoid confusion, however, the reader must remember that employee income did not show a big rise in this period. It was a depression and employees were hurting. Their share of national income rose only because there was a catastrophic decline of profit.

In the last five cycles from 1970 to 2001, the decline of the employee share in expansions was much greater than its rise in recessions. Thus the long-run effect was a decline in the employee share of income from 1970 to 2001. Similarly, the decline in the employee share in the Bush expansion was much greater than the average decline in the previous five cycles.

## Why the Employee Share Falls in Most of the Expansion

The employee share of national income usually falls in the first four stages of the expansion, and then rises a little in the last stage. The immediate reason for the fall in the employee share in most of the expansion is that employee income rises very little at first, then slowly for the rest of the expansion. But property income, especially corporate profit, rises very rapidly in the first four stages. Thus the share of employees must fall in that period. And it always does.

Why does employee income rise so slowly in expansions? In the beginning of the recovery phase of the cycle, there are still large numbers of unemployed workers and professionals willing to take new jobs at relatively low pay. In the average recovery, the bargaining power of employees and unions is relatively weak for reasons discussed below.

When unions have a small percentage of the labor force, the bargaining power of employees is weakened. The weakness of unions and employees in the early expansion is caused in part by the existence of a reserve army of unemployed workers, left over from the previous recession.

Another reason for the weakness of employees in the early recovery is the public attitude toward changes in employee income. The public is sympathetic to employees resisting cuts in employee compensation. The public, however, has little sympathy for fights for increases in wages and salaries. Even employees are more easily aroused to anger and militancy to resist wage cuts than they are enthusiastic to strike for wage or salary increases. Another factor that prevents unions and employees from raising wages or salaries is the existence of contracts with fixed wages and salaries for a two- or three-year period.

In early expansion, the big profit increases come primarily from increased productivity of labor and machines. To be more specific, large profit increases result partly from investment in new machinery. New machinery increases the productivity of employees and lessens the need to hire more employees.

Another reason for profit increases is that, in the recession, factories were using a low percentage of their total equipment. In the early recovery, they started to increase their use of the equipment they own. The organization and use of labor and machines become more efficient when a somewhat higher level of production is reached for which the factory was designed.

Finally, in an expansion every increase in output tends to cause an equal increase in the number of production-line workers. But some kinds of non-production-line workers need not be increased. For example, the number of security guards and bookkeepers need not be increased as fast as production increases. So corporations can hire fewer workers per unit of output and their profit margins will rise.

Why do wages and salaries usually keep rising in the expansion, but much slower than output? Unions and employees gain greater bargaining power when more employees are needed. Employee militancy also increases as employees become fully aware of productivity increases and soaring profit.

Nevertheless, under capitalism the increasing production does not automatically benefit the employees. They must bargain, or even strike, for higher wages and salaries. So, since the strength of employees is almost always less than the strength of corporations, their wages and salaries rise but more slowly than profit in an expansion.

## Why Does the Employee Share Rise in the Last Stage of Expansion?

The slight rise in the employee share in the last stage of expansion does *not* mean that employees are suddenly getting a lot more income. On the contrary, their income increase is tiny, if anything. So how can their share of national income rise? The simple answer is that profit starts to fall in the last stage of expansion. Since wages are steady, while profit is falling, the employee share rises.

These facts have some important consequences and offer several clues for the decline into recession or depression. Since wages and salaries are not actually rising in the last stage of expansion, neither does consumer demand for the products of business. The next chapter explains that this is one cause of recession, so it is very important as a clue to the roller coaster.

A later chapter will explain why profit falls in the last stage of expansion.

## Why Does the Employee Share Rise in a Recession?

This is an easy question. Wages and salaries go down to some extent in a recession, and they go way down in a depression. Thus the income of those employees who are now unemployed declines disastrously. Therefore the living standard of employees goes way down and there is widespread misery. So if employee income goes way down in a depression, why does the employee share increase?

The answer is very clear. Profit goes down very fast even in a recession. In the Great Depression, aggregate corporate profit of the United States was negative for several years. If wages and salaries are very low, but corporations actually have negative profits, then obviously the employee share rises. But it is a bigger share of a much tinier pie. Moreover, employees' living standards will still be far below the living standards of the millionaires and billionaires.

## Conclusions About Income in the Last Five Cycles

What conclusions should be drawn from these five cycles concerning the changing income distribution and its effect on the roller coaster economy? In every expansion, employee incomes rise very slowly, while corporate profit rises rapidly. For this reason, the ratio of employee income to national income declines for most of the expansion. The opposite behavior occurs in every recession.

The fact that the employee share of income falls in expansions and rises in contractions will turn out to be an important clue to unravel the mystery of recessions and depressions. The next chapter will show its significance.

## The Bush Expansion, 2001 to 2007

As shown above, in the average expansion, the employee share of national income falls in most of the expansion, rising slightly only at the end. This pattern continued in the Bush expansion, but the increasing income gap between employee income and national income becomes clearer by focusing on employee versus profit income.

For the Bush expansion, the data show the difference between the growth of employee income and the growth of corporate profit in each year of the expansion. The difference is very clear in Figure 4.3.

Figure 4.3 shows that corporate profit declined in the recession of 2001. After that, in the Bush expansion, corporate profit increased its pace of growth to an astonishing degree. In mid-expansion, corporate profit rose 20 percent in 2004. (To make the comparison as clear as possible, the data in this graph are direct from the source and not corrected for taxes or inflation.)

In the last half of the Bush expansion, profit grew slower and slower. Notice that Chapter 3 found the same pattern of declining growth in GDP in the last half of the Bush expansion. Only when the recession influenced the annual data in 2007 was there a slight decline in corporate profit on an annual basis (but the picture emerges differently in the quarterly data discussed below.)

Employee income grew less than corporate profits every year except 2001 during the recession, when profit actually fell. In the first three years, employee income grew at a snail's pace. In the rest of the expansion, employee income grew at a slow but steady pace that never approached the rate at which corporate profits expanded. Thus, as in every postwar expansion, profits grew far faster than wages, salaries, and benefits. The difference from previous expansions was that the gap between the slow rise of wages and salaries and the extraordinary rise of profit was enormous in the Bush expansion.

Figure 4.3  **Employee Income and Corporate Profit by Year, 2001–2007**

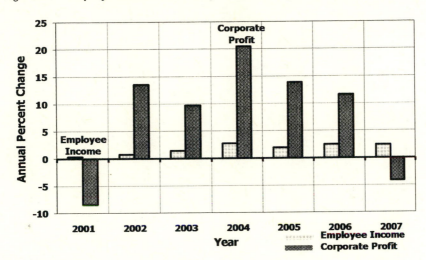

*Source:* Bureau of Economic Analysis, Department of Commerce (www.bea.gov).
*Note:* Employee income is all wages, salaries, and benefits. Profit is corporate profit before taxes. Percent change, year-to-year, 2001 to 2007, in billions of actual dollars.

The next chapter will show that the increasing gap between profit and employee income is a very powerful clue to explain the behavior of consumer spending. Thus, this gap is a major key to the unraveling of the mystery of why an expansion ever ends and a recession or depression begins.

## Income in the Great Recession, 2007 to 2009

The Great Recession began in the fourth quarter of 2007 and continued its economic contraction into 2009. The financial crisis, which was part of the Great Recession, became a panic in the fourth quarter of 2008. For this reason employee income and corporate profit both fell in 2007 and 2008, but the biggest decline was in the fourth quarter of 2008. Figure 4.4 makes these movements clear.

Corporate profit declined in the third and fourth quarters of 2007. Corporate profit continued to decline throughout 2008. Profit suddenly hurtled downward at a 50 percent annual rate in the fourth quarter.

Employee income (before correction for taxes and inflation) continued to rise in 2007 and 2008. Employee income, however, rose more and more slowly. Employee income finally fell in the fourth quarter. At the same time, GDP fell over 6 percent and corporate profit fell 50 percent! The level of

Figure 4.4 **Employee Income and Corporate Profit in the Crisis, 2007.4–2008.4**

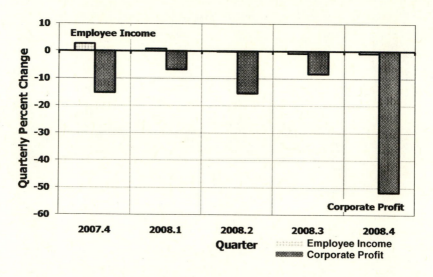

*Source:* Bureau of Economic Analysis, Department of Commerce (www.bea.gov).
*Note:* Employee income is all wages, salaries, and benefits. Profit is corporate profits before taxes. Percent change, quarter-to-quarter, 2007.4 to 2008.4, in billions of actual dollars, seasonally adjusted.

employee income (uncorrected for inflation and taxes) has seldom fallen for even a quarter in all of the recessions since the Great Depression.

When employee income falls, it sets up a vicious circle in the economy. The vicious circle of the Great Recession went this way. Less employment leads to less aggregate employee income. Less income leads to less spending. Less spending means fewer sales and profits across the economy. The story begins again when less sales lead to less employment. Every unemployed person means a further reduction of consumer spending.

Why did the vicious circle accelerate downward? When millions of employees, from low paid to high paid were fired in 2007, this had to lead to less consumer spending. In late 2008 and early 2009, every day of the week witnessed thousands of people being fired. Every day of the week, one could see that less and less people brought home paychecks. Lost income meant less spending, as will be seen in the next chapter. Lower consumer spending leads to less profit, less production, and more employees being fired.

**Clues to Remember**

First, there is an extremely high level of inequality in the United States between the rich and the poor, as well as between employees and corporate owners.

Second, from 1970 to the present, the degree of inequality in the United States has greatly increased between rich and poor as well as between employees and corporate owners.

Third, in every business cycle expansion, the degree of inequality between employees and corporate owners increases. In other words, in every expansion, and with special force in the Bush expansion, aggregate employee income falls behind corporate profits. As a result, the employee share of national income falls throughout the expansion until profit begins to fall on the eve of the recession. In every recession, profit falls very rapidly, while employee income falls more slowly.

**Suggested Reading**

An explanation in simple terms of the effect of the global economy on American workers is Robert Pollin's "Global Outsourcing and the U.S. Working Class," *New Labor Forum* 16, no. 1 (2007): 122–125.

# 5

# The Consumption Gap

The largest single element of expenditures in the U.S. economy comes from the American consumer. Consumer spending was the Energizer Bunny that kept the economy growing through the 1990s and for the first seven years of this century. After that expansion, however, the Great Recession of 2007 to 2009 witnessed the disastrous economic consequences of what happens when consumers cut back on spending.

When consumption is cut back below its peak, it creates a consumption gap. In other words, it is the gap between the possible production of goods and services for people to use and the actual production of goods and services under the present economic system. In the Great Recession of 2007 to 2009, the actual production was held down by the lack of demand from paying customers. In the U.S. economic system, the desires and the needs of consumers, if they cannot pay money for goods and services, do not count.

**Structural Change in Consumer Demand**

Long ago, in the 1950s and 1960s, employee income from wages and salaries rose almost every year by a significant amount. As a result, consumer spending rose most years by a significant amount.

In the early 1970s, however, changes in the global economy changed all that. For one thing, other countries began to catch up with the United States, so the U.S. share of world production and trade began to fall. Due to that competition and the weakening of labor unions by various means, real wages and salaries showed very little growth from then till now.

Since employee income is the largest source of consumer spending, there was a big decline over the decades in the growth rate of consumer spending. It will be shown in detail in this chapter that the weakened growth of consumer spending was one of the major causes of the Great Recession of 2007 and the country's inability to recover from the downturn in 2008 and 2009.

## What Decides How Much Consumers Spend?

Most consumers spend all of their income, so there is little or no personal saving for the average consumer. Sometimes consumers cannot buy what they need from their income. Then they borrow, which is discussed below.

Most consumer income comes from wages and salaries. Since the growth of that income has been very slight for decades, consumer spending rises very slowly, even in expansions.

## Consumer Spending Over the Cycle 1970 to 2001

How does aggregate (total) consumer spending actually behave in each expansion and in each recession? As a background to the Bush expansion and recession, consumption is examined in the previous five cycles, from 1970 to 2001. Figure 5.1 shows what happened on the average.

Consumption in this graph is defined as real, meaning that the movements of consumer spending have been corrected according to the amount of price inflation. Real data give a clearer picture of what happens if the buying power of a single dollar is held constant. If the data include inflation, consumption would appear to just keep rising all the time.

What does Figure 5.1 show? Real consumption rose at a moderate pace for the first four stages of the expansion. In the last stage before the peak, consumption grew more slowly. In the recession, the real amount of consumer goods and services actually declined only a little during the mostly mild recessions from 1970 to 2001. Consumption began to pick up again only in the last stage of the recession.

The question is why consumer spending behaves this way over the business cycle. As mentioned earlier, consumer spending in an expansion generally just equals consumer income.

That sounds simple, but average spending hides the fact that it is composed of the spending of two groups acting very differently. One group, the owners of corporations, saves in the form of shares of the corporations. Corporations also save some of corporate income as retained corporate profit that is never paid out to the shareholders. The other group, the employees, does not save. The aggregate of all employees rather goes deeper into debt each year of the expansion. If the income of these two groups is added together, then aggregate consumer income is almost all spent for goods and services in the expansion and there is almost no aggregate personal saving.

Figure 5.1 **Consumer Spending by Cycle, 1970–2001**

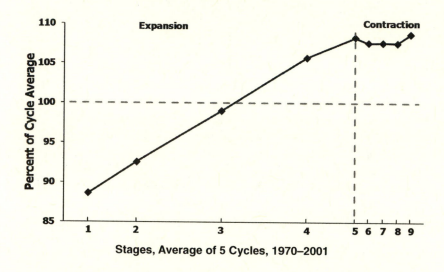

Stages, Average of 5 Cycles, 1970–2001

*Source:* Department of Commerce, Bureau of Economic Analysis (www.bea.gov).
*Note:* Consumer spending is aggregate consumer expenditures. Average of five cycles,
1970 to 2001, in billions of chained 2000 dollars, seasonally adjusted quarterly data.

## Employee Income and Consumer Spending

The previous chapter found that the share of employees (their wages and
salaries and benefits) in national income falls in much of the expansion. The
rest of national income goes to property income (profit, rent, and interest), so
the share of property income must rise through much of the expansion.

Whether you cheer for employees or for the business owners, the point is
that this change from employee income to the profit income of business has
a major effect on aggregate consumer spending.

Why is that? Profit income goes mainly to the rich. So the receivers of
profit are able to have a high level of consumption, yet also save some of
their profit. In other words, if their income is $950,000 a year, an increase
to $1 million a year does not mean so much to them. They may choose not
to increase their consumer spending at all, but put all the money saved into
the stock market.

Employees have to spend all or most of their income just to keep what
is considered a moderate living standard. If they earn $25,000 a year, they
may decide they have to spend all of an increase of $2,000 a year to pay for
food, clothing, and shelter. Therefore, they can save none of it. Thus the ratio

of consumers' spending to their income remains very high for the average employee even when the economy expands.

In fact, most employees today cannot survive at a reasonable level without going into debt. They use more and more credit to finance their family's survival on limited consumer goods and services. The gap between the income and the spending of the average person is filled more and more by credit, as shown below.

Although there is little personal saving, corporations save part of their profits. This part is not paid out to share holders, so it never becomes personal income.

Those corporate savings are also owned by the shareholders. When corporate saving is added to individual capitalist saving, then capitalists do save a considerable amount. As the expansion gains speed, the capitalist owners and their corporations do save a higher proportion of all corporate income.

So what happens when there is an expansion with a falling share of national income going to employees and a rising share going to capitalist owners? The economy has shifted income away from employees who spend all their income on consumption (and go into debt to spend more) to capitalist owners of industry. These capitalist owners and their corporations save more and more income as the expansion continues.

When the growth of employee income slows, the growth of consumer spending on goods and services also slows.

This is an important clue to the mystery of why the expansion does not go on forever. Here, slowing growth of consumption is one important factor in the slowing of the whole economy. Remember that consumer spending is the largest single element of spending. If it slows, so does the revenue of corporations.

The "consumer share" is defined as the percentage that consumers spend out of the national income. At the end of the expansion, the wealthy capitalist class put a higher proportion of its income into the stock market. Moreover, national income also includes some income that just stays with corporations, all of which is saved and not spent for consumption. The result of a reduced employee share is that, for every dollar of income, less will be spent on consumption. In other words, the consumer share must fall toward the end of every expansion.

This decline in the share of consumer spending out of national income means that a gap opens between consumer demand and the supply of consumer goods. As consumer spending rises more slowly, this gap becomes an important factor reducing overall demand for the national product of the United States. It is one of the factors, an important one, leading to recession.

## Consumer Share and Employee Share

Employee income, which is mainly wages and salaries, is by far the largest single income source for consumer demand. Naturally, aggregate consumption and aggregate employee income tend to move together. Similarly, the consumer share of national income and the employee share of national income march together through the cycle. The consumer share and the employee share over the business cycle are compared in Figure 5.2.

Chapter 4 discussed the employee share and its cyclical ups and downs. The employee share generally falls in expansions and rises in contractions. In the average of the last five cycles, as Figure 5.2 shows, the employee share fell in the first four stages of expansion. But it rose slightly just before the economy declined. It continued to rise throughout the recession.

The previous chapter explained at length why the employee share falls during most of the expansion. The slight rise at the end of expansion happens because employee income continues to rise very slowly, but profit falls in the last stage of expansion (for reasons discussed later).

Figure 5.2 also depicts the consumer share. The figure reveals that the consumer share mostly follows the same direction as the employee share. Thus, the consumer share generally falls in expansions and rises in contractions. In the average of the last five cycles, Figure 5.2 shows that it fell in the first four stages of expansion. But it rose slightly just before the economy declined. It continued to rise throughout the recession.

Figure 5.2 indicates that the decline in the employee share of national income in most of the expansion is a major cause of the decline of the consumer share in most of the expansion. Whenever the employee share rises, so does the consumer share. Whenever the employee share falls, the consumer share falls. In other words, when the income of most of the populace grows at a slower pace than previously, their consumption also grows at a slower pace. Here, therefore, is the first set of clues as to why expansions end in crises and recessions. Employee income rises more slowly than in mid-expansion. Then consumer spending also rises more slowly than in mid-expansion. Of course, consumers have the same need and desire for goods and services, but they have less money to spend as a percentage share of the consumer goods and services that are offered. That increasing consumption gap has an effect on the economy. The gap means less revenue for corporations, so it is one of the major causes of every economic disaster.

## What Does the Consumer Share Do in Recessions?

Let us briefly review what has been said about the expansion, and then look at the recession. Employee income and total consumer spending rise throughout the

Figure 5.2 **Consumer Share and Employee Share by Cycle, 1970–2001**

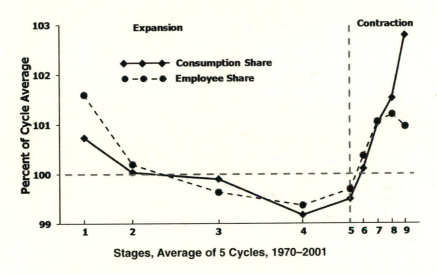

**Stages, Average of 5 Cycles, 1970–2001**

*Source:* Department of Commerce, Bureau of Economic Analysis (www.bea.gov).
*Note:* Employee share is the ratio of employee compensation to national income. Consumption share is the ratio of consumption to national income. Both series are average of five cycles, 1970 to 2001, in billions of chained 2000 dollars, seasonally adjusted quarterly data.

expansion up to the cycle peak. But the share of employee income and of consumer spending in the national income both fall for the first four stages of the cycle.

That decline is very important because it slows the growth of consumer spending up to that time. The slower growth of consumer spending means less revenue for business. It therefore tends to lower corporate profit. It is one of the reasons that corporate profit begins to fall in the last stage of the expansion—and continues to fall in the recession.

In the last stage of expansion, wages and salaries are still rising a little, but total business profit is falling. Therefore, the share of employees in national income rises a little. Through most of the recession, employee income falls. But profits fall even faster. Therefore, even though employees are hurting badly from unemployment and falling wages and salaries, their share of national income continues to rise for most of the recession.

The tale of the consumer share is similar. In the last stage of the expansion, total consumer spending continues to rise, though slowly. But because profit outlook has dimmed (as shown in Chapter 7), the amount that corporations are willing to invest slows even more than consumption. Thus the consumer share shows a slight rise in the last stage of expansion.

Throughout the recession, the consumer share continues to rise for the same reason. Total consumption falls, but not as fast as total investment falls. Eventually, toward the end of the recession, as consumption falls more and more slowly, it may help set the stage for recovery.

## Consumer Credit

Although change in employee income is the major factor affecting consumer spending, other causes are also examined below.

Consumers get credit by going into debt to financial companies. In the average cycle from 1970 to 2001, credit rose enormously in the expansion, and then declined a tiny bit in the recession. The increase of credit helped postpone each recession. The large amount of outstanding credit, however, made each recession worse than it would otherwise have been because people and businesses could not pay back the money they owed. The result was bankruptcy and foreclosure of mortgages. The fact that the money could not be repaid caused damage to the financial companies, which made the recessions worse.

In Chapter 8, the powerful role of consumer credit in the expansion of 2001 to 2007 and in the Great Recession and financial crisis of 2007 to 2009 will be traced in detail.

## The Wealth Effect

The average capitalist owners have large incomes, putting them into the top 1 percent of income receivers. Some of that income is spent on consumer goods and services, but some of it is saved. Those savings are used in part to invest in corporations or other businesses. A small percentage is kept as cash savings accounts in banks, which is not spent until a later time; and some goes into speculative investments. One type of speculative investment is buying assets, such as stock, from other people. This transfer of stock does not increase the physical amount of business investment in equipment or buildings; it merely changes the ownership. Another speculative investment is buying a house if it is purely for the purpose of reselling it at a higher price, rather than living in it. Thus employees spend all their income on consumer goods and services. Capitalists, however, still have money left over after a high level of consumer spending, so they do other things with the remainder.

In addition to income and credit, consumer behavior is influenced by the amount of wealth a person holds. There is a distinction between wealth and income. Income is the amount of money a person earns in a year. Wealth is the amount that an individual has managed to save over a lifetime. Wealth may be held in the form of cash or bank deposits or home ownership or corporate stock or anything else convertible to money.

For most people, the effect of wealth on spending has little importance. Many people have little or no net wealth after debts are subtracted. Only among the richest citizens of America is there enough wealth to make its rise or decline important.

Homeowners own some equity in their home. Equity in a home means the value of the home minus the mortgage, which is the money borrowed to buy the home. If homeowners do own equity, they feel richer as long as their home's value is rising. For example, in the long real estate bubble ending in 2006, millions of people thought they were getting richer. Therefore, they felt comfortable spending more of their income on consumer goods and services. When the bubble broke, house prices declined rapidly, so these people felt much poorer. As a result, they spent less on consumer goods and services.

So, early in the long expansion of the 1990s, stock prices went up and up till they also were in a bubble in which they were far above any realistic value. When the expansion ended in 2001, stock prices declined a whole 50 percent to the bottom in 2003. During that huge slide of the value of stocks, even the well to do who held stocks felt poorer and poorer. Therefore, some of them also reduced their buying of consumer goods and services.

In brief, if the value of what they own in a house or stock or anything else rises, people spend more on consumer goods and services. If the value of their house or stock or other assets declines, they spend less on consumer goods and services. This is the wealth effect.

It should be emphasized that the so-called wealth effect struck the average person even more than the rich in the financial crisis of 2008. This is because everyone with a house and a mortgage was threatened. Millions of people had bought houses on credit through mortgages, and often got more money by increasing the mortgage. They used the new credit to pay debts and to maintain their standard of living. But when it began to look like they might lose their houses to foreclosure, they drastically cut back on their consumer spending, feeling that they had no choice.

### Conclusions on Consumption, 1970 to 2001

Aggregate consumer spending has risen in recent decades, but at a slower and slower rate per decade. Wages and salaries have risen more slowly than profit; and consumer debt has risen faster than consumer income.

In the average business cycle of the last four decades, consumer spending has risen in every expansion, though slower as the peak is approached.

Consumer spending rose in the expansion more slowly than national income, so the consumption share fell in the expansion.

In recessions, everything was reversed. Consumption fell slowly, so it did not fall as much as national income. The consumer share of national income rose in recessions.

Wages and salaries are the most important source of consumer spending. But wages and salaries do not rise as fast as national income. This is one reason why consumer spending rose more slowly than national income.

On the contrary, in a recession, wages and salaries fall more slowly than national income. Therefore, this is one reason that consumer spending falls more slowly than national income.

This chapter revealed that the consumer share and the employee share move downward together during each business expansion (until the last stage of expansion), but they move upward together to some extent during recessions.

Another factor affecting consumption is the rising tide of consumer credit and debt. In expansions, increasing consumer credit helps maintain the expansion a little longer. But when there is a crisis or recession, consumers face a mountain of debt. Many consumers are forced to default on their debts through bankruptcy. Many are also forced to lose their houses through foreclosure. Consumer bankruptcy and foreclosures reduce their actual buying power, as well as their perception of what is safe to borrow or spend.

**Consumption in the Expansion, 2001 to 2007**

The same consumer behavior is found in the Bush expansion of 2001 to 2007, but the trends were more extreme. As shown in earlier chapters, the Bush expansion was weak, with a lower growth rate than the previous average. Moreover, the gap between the growth rate of employee income and corporate profit was enormous.

With less and less of the national income, employees had less to spend on consumption. They used an increasing amount of credit to fill the gap. Yet even with credit, the weak recovery—plus the very weak growth of jobs and employee income—resulted in a very slow growth of consumption compared with earlier cycles. These trends can be seen in Figure 5.3.

Figure 5.3 shows that consumption during the Bush expansion moved upward rapidly in the first half of the expansion. Its highest growth rate was reached in the middle of the expansion. After reaching a peak growth rate in 2004, consumer spending rose more and more slowly up to the peak of the expansion in 2007. This is the same pattern displayed by GDP as seen in Chapter 3.

The slower growth of consumer spending, down to a much lower growth

Figure 5.3 **Consumer Spending by Year, 2001–2007**

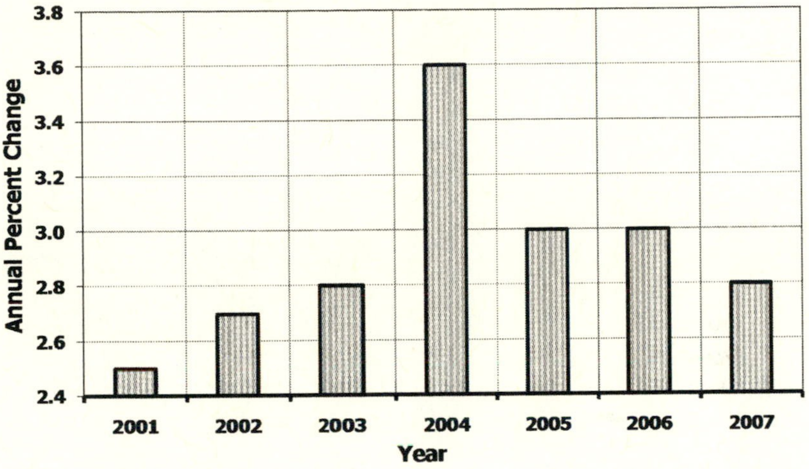

*Source:* Bureau of Economic Analysis, Department of Commerce (www.bea.gov).
*Note:* Consumer spending, percent change, year to year.

by the end, was one factor leading to the Great Recession, which began in the fourth quarter of 2007. Thus, the consumer gap not only means less consumption for individuals, but also poses an increasing danger to the economy. It was not the only danger, but it was an important one.

### Consumption in the Crisis, 2007 to 2009

What happened to consumer spending from the beginning of the Great Recession in the last quarter of 2007 through the financial panic in the last quarter of 2008? The answer is shown in Figure 5.4.

As usual, consumers attempted to carry on in the Great Recession as they had been doing in the late expansion. For the first three quarters of the Great Recession, consumers managed to continue the slow growth pace. How did they do that when people were beginning to lose their jobs? Those with savings dug into their savings to pay the bills. Those who had no savings resorted to an increase in their credit. If they could get credit no other way, some people took out a larger mortgage. Somehow the average consumer kept up almost the same standard of living for some time in the crisis.

In the last two quarters of 2008, however, the Great Recession became apparent to everyone. Job losses became enormous, and large numbers of employees were being fired every day. Finally, by the fourth quarter of 2008,

Figure 5.4 **Consumer Spending in the Crisis, 2007.4–2008.4**

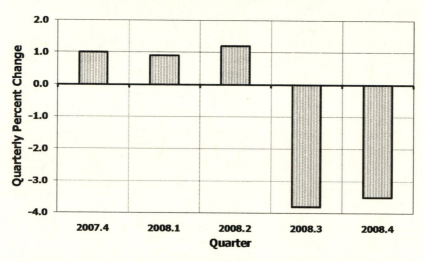

*Source:* Bureau of Economic Analysis, Department of Commerce (www.bea.gov).
*Note:* Consumer spending, percent change, quarter to quarter.

there was a freeze on credit. The freeze meant that almost no one could borrow, regardless of their income. Since people were losing their jobs and were unable to get credit, they were forced to reduce their consumption. There was a large decline in aggregate consumption. People reduced every kind of spending, from children's toys to medically prescribed drugs.

Such a slowing of consumption growth, followed by a large two-quarter decline, had been unknown since the Great Depression. This event provides another clue toward a solution of the mystery of the onset of the Great Recession.

Notice the vicious circle. Consumption growth declines. Jobs decline. Fewer people can spend the same amount of money on consumer goods and services, so consumption declines strongly. This is followed by even larger job losses. It was obvious that the Great Recession was spreading throughout the whole economy and deepening at an accelerated pace.

**Clues to Remember**

First, personal saving disappeared before the Great Recession. Saving was in the form of profit retained by the corporation and owned by shareholders.

Second, during most of the expansion, the consumer share declined while corporate profit rose.

Third, the movements of the consumer share and the employee share over the business cycle were closely related. They fell together in expansion and they rose together in contraction.

Fourth, when credit dried up and more and more people lost their jobs in the second half of 2008, the resulting collapse of consumption pushed the economy into the Great Recession.

# 6

# The Housing Crisis

As this chapter is being written, the U.S. economy is in the grip of a virulent housing crisis. In this crisis, housing construction is declining, housing prices are falling, and foreclosures are skyrocketing. The crisis is hurting people and it is hurting the rest of the economy. How did this happen?

**Structural Change in Housing**

In the 1950s and 1960s, average income rose year to year. More and more middle-income employees bought homes. From the 1970s to the present, however, average employee income stagnated, so workers did not have enough to buy a house. They used credit to fill the gap. After 2006, however, many people could not pay their mortgages and millions lost their homes. This chapter explores how this happened.

**The Housing Cycle**

The housing cycle has the same general causes as the cycle in the economy as a whole. The two cycles strongly influence each other. Nevertheless, the housing cycle often has peaks and troughs at different times than the general cycle. In addition, the rate of construction of housing rises and falls at a different pace than the other sectors of the economy.

There is a large literature on the housing cycle (see discussion of sources in Sherman 1991, Chapter 5). In most of the recorded data, researchers found a cycle in housing of as much as fifteen years, with seven- or eight-year expansions and seven- or eight-year contractions. The longer housing cycle has continued to the present. For example, housing prices reached a low point in about 1995, then soared straight upward till about 2006. This great growth continued in spite of the 2001 recession. This bubble in housing construction and housing prices was one cause of the economic crisis of 2008.

Why do housing construction and home prices usually have a cycle longer than other sectors of the economy? Suppose the economic outlook appears rosy to many people. Homebuilders start the process of expanding residential construction. First, they must get architectural plans. Then they must get loans. Then they usually need to get local government approval based on the zoning laws for the location where they wish to build. Then they start building. The construction of a large building or a housing tract may take years, and the builders are expending money over that whole time. As a result, there is a long time lag from the first idea of building homes until the last dollar is spent.

There are also many time lags when a decline of housing begins before it all can work its course. One major reason is that many projects are still in process when a downturn begins. So despite a housing decline, many construction sites would still be functioning. These must all be finished and on the market before it is possible to begin to reduce the number of housing units for sale. Housing construction and sales, therefore, do have a cycle of expansion and contraction, but these cycles often do not coincide with the business cycle.

Housing construction does decline in more severe contractions, but often continues to rise in mild recessions. The purchase of housing in the housing cycle can be compared with the purchase of equipment in the general business cycle. Purchase of new equipment reflects the business investment decision, so it is at the heart of the cycle. On the contrary, residential housing is mostly bought by people who wish to live in it. Houses are not used like business equipment, to produce anything else. Rather houses provide a service for those who live in them. Except for speculators, most people buy a house as they buy other durable consumer goods, as a thing that is useful for living, so it does not behave like a business investment.

In the happier period of 1949 to 1970, economic performance was good and recessions were mild. Business investment in equipment rose 30 percent in expansions, but fell only 12 percent in contractions. Housing construction behaved more like consumer spending. During business cycle expansions, housing construction rose only 7 percent, but continued to rise in contractions by another 3 percent. So it appears that housing grew slowly, but continuously, though a little slower during contractions. During the long existence of the housing bubble, most people thought housing prices would climb forever.

## Housing in the Five Cycles, 1970 to 2001

In the last five cycles, from 1970 to 2001, what happened can be best seen in a picture of the behavior of housing construction. Figure 6.1 shows the cyclical behavior of housing construction for this period.

Figure 6.1  **Housing Construction by Cycle, 1970–2001**

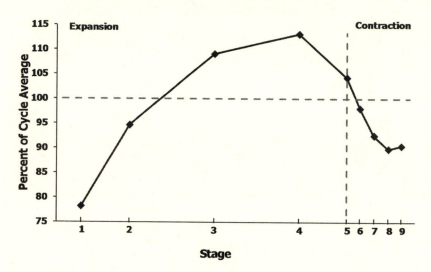

*Source:* Bureau of Economic Analysis, Department of Commerce (www.bea.gov).
*Note:* Housing construction is defined as real residential private domestic investment, averaged over five cycles, 1970.4 to 2001.4, in billions of chained 2000 dollars, seasonally adjusted quarterly data.

Figure 6.1 shows housing construction, which is called "residential investment" by the government. Housing construction behaved similarly to GDP and consumption during much of the expansion. Housing construction rose rapidly in the early recovery; then it continued to rise more and more slowly until the stage before the peak.

In the last stage of expansion, however, housing construction declined. Thus housing led GDP and consumption. Thus the decline in housing in the last stage of expansion was one of the factors that usually helped to bring on the recession. That leading influence was true of the average of the five expansions, but it was also true in the Bush expansion. It helped the expansion, but it was also one of the villains causing the recession.

In the average recession of the last five cycles, housing construction declined for most of the recession. But in the last stage of the recession, housing construction moved upward a little. It was one of the factors helping to start a recovery. So, in this period, housing construction was a leading indicator of the cycle, turning down before the cycle peak and turning upward before the cycle trough.

This average behavior should not be relied upon because there is a wide variation in the behavior of housing construction from cycle to cycle. When

Figure 6.2 **Housing Prices by Cycle, 1970–2001**

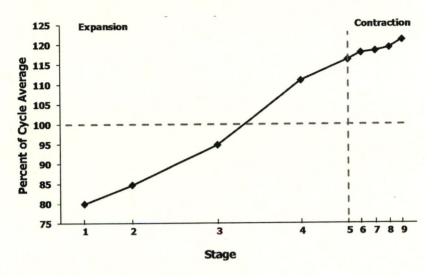

Source: U.S. Census Bureau (www.census.gov).
*Note:* Price of houses sold, average cycle pattern over five cycles, 1970 to 2001, in current dollars.

it does decline in an expansion or rise in the contraction, however, a wise observer will watch more carefully for a turn in the whole cycle.

## Housing Prices Over the Cycle 1970 to 2001

What about the price of housing in the last five cycles from 1970 to 2001? The average story is told in Figure 6.2, which reveals that, in the average of the previous five cycles, the price of houses rose during the average expansion of the economy. But unlike GDP, it did not have lower growth over the last half of expansion. It just kept rising at about the same rate.

Moreover, GDP fell in the average recession. But housing prices continued to rise, though more slowly, in the average recession of the period from 1970 to 2001. Since all the recessions from 1949 to 2001 were relatively mild, housing prices rose on average in most periods. In the recession of 2001, housing construction and prices slowed only a little. Housing was a factor in helping to recover from recession and helping to prevent a Great Recession.

It is impossible to overemphasize the boom in housing prices over the last four decades. Such a continuous rise, in both business expansions and business contractions, has no equal in the last 150 years of record keeping. It was

Figure 6.3  **Housing Construction by Year, 2001–2007**

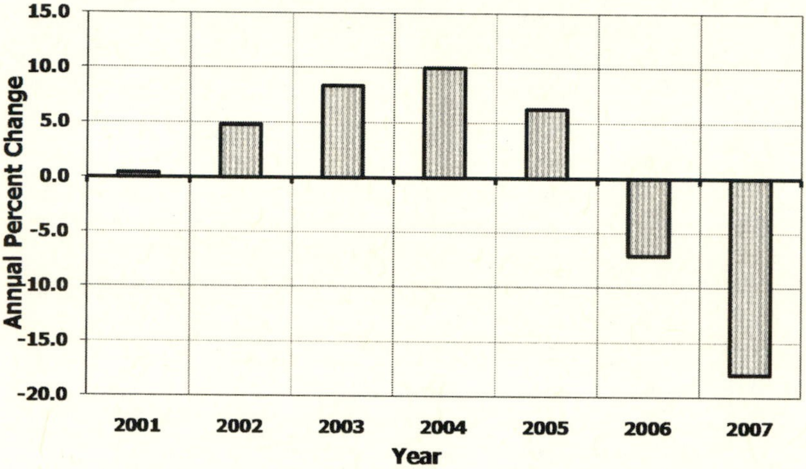

Source: Bureau of Economic Analysis, Department of Commerce (www.bea.gov).
  *Note:* Housing construction is defined as real residential private domestic investment, percent change, year to year, 2001 to 2007, in billions of chained 2000 dollars, seasonally adjusted.

an extraordinary rise that could certainly be called a bubble. When economic bubbles disappear, the collapse is usually extreme.

## Housing Construction in the Expansion, 2001 to 2007

What happened to housing in the expansion of 2001 to 2007? The path of housing construction in the expansion is shown in Figure 6.3. The graph reveals that housing construction rose a tiny bit even in the recession year of 2001. Then it continued to rise faster and faster, reaching about 10 percent growth in 2004 in the mid-expansion. It was a bright spot in the recovery and helped to raise the general rate of growth during a weak recovery. In 2005 it still agreed with GDP and consumption in that it continued to grow, but more slowly.

In the last two years of the expansion, however, it deviated strongly from other sectors. The long rapid growth and the bubble in housing were over. Housing construction began its decline in 2006. It led the cycle by a considerable amount, falling while the expansion continued. In comparison with the last five cycles, it fell much sooner in the expansion and fell much stronger than in the earlier cycles. It was perhaps the major contributor to the business cycle contraction that began at the end of 2007.

74

Figure 6.4  **Housing Prices by Year, 2001–2007**

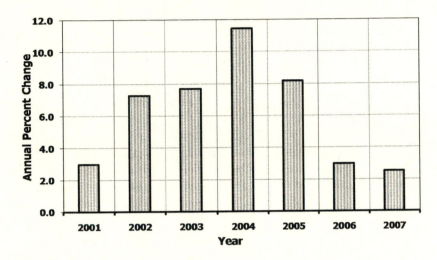

*Source:* U.S. Census Bureau (www.census.gov).
*Note:* Sales price of houses sold, percent change, year to year, 2001 to 2007, in current dollars.

In fact, as Chapter 8 will show, the decline of housing construction, the fall in housing prices, and the great increase in foreclosures set off the financial crisis. It was not the sole cause of that crisis by any means, but it pushed a steadily weakening and increasingly fragile financial structure over the brink.

## Housing Prices in the Expansion, 2001 to 2007

Housing prices and housing construction are two different things. They usually move together as demand moves up or down, but at different paces and somewhat different times. Housing prices are depicted in Figure 6.4 showing that they went slowly upward in 2001, even though it was a recession year. The bubble in housing prices then continued to grow rapidly until it reached almost 12 percent annual growth in 2004. At that point, housing prices began to weaken. There were three years of slower and slower growth of housing prices. Housing prices rose at a slow crawl up to the cycle peak, and then fell precipitously during the recession.

As noted above, housing construction actually declined in the last two years of the Bush expansion. The slower growth of the housing price bubble reflected a weaker housing sector. Demand for housing was weakening. Chapter 4

Figure 6.5 **Housing Construction in the Crisis, 2007.4–2008.4**

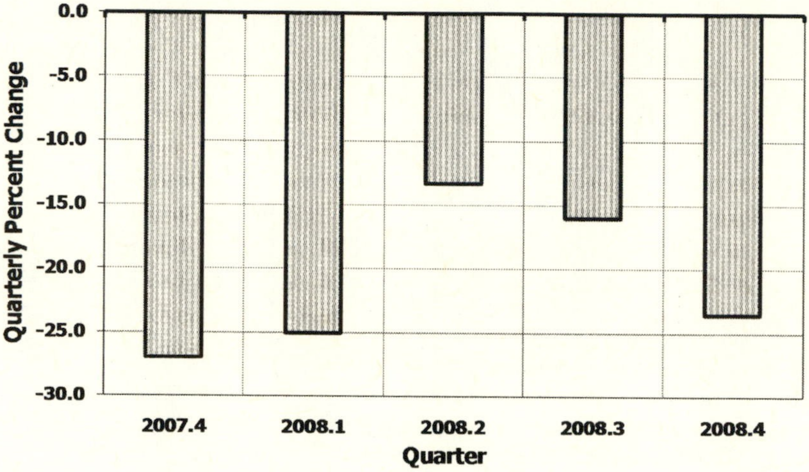

*Source:* Bureau of Economic Analysis, Department of Commerce (www.bea.gov).
*Note:* Residential construction is defined as real residential private domestic investment, percent change, quarter to quarter, 2007.4 to 2008.4, in billions of chained 2000 dollars, seasonally adjusted quarterly data, at annual rates.

showed that the income of the average employee was rising very, very slowly by that time. Rising prices in other sectors, such as health care, were eating up more of the family budget. Little was left for spending on houses. Most of the houses were bought with credit. The home loans, guaranteed by mortgages, were supported by less and less available income among the middle-income group. This important clue will be followed up in Chapter 8 on credit.

## Housing Construction in the Great Recession, 2007 to 2009

As shown above, housing construction led the way down in the period before the Great Recession began in the fourth quarter of 2007. What happened next is shown in Figure 6.5, which shows that in the first half year of the recession housing construction fell at a very rapid pace. The average decline was at a rate of about 25 percent a year. This strong decline began before GDP or most of the economy had fallen very far, so housing was still a downward leader.

The main reason for the housing decline was that the average person, a middle-income employee, lacked the money to buy a home at the inflated, bubble prices. Now the situation had worsened because many employees had lost their jobs. Furthermore, banks were becoming afraid to lend much credit through mortgages because it finally dawned on them that this was a very risky market.

One important indicator of the risk being taken was the rise in the number of subprime mortgages. A prime mortgage is a loan on a house in which the borrower has a very high credit rating, showing that the borrower can easily repay the loan. A subprime mortgage is a loan on a house in which the borrower has less funds and lower income than the bank considers safe for making a loan.

In the expansion of 2001 to 2007, however, banks and other lenders assumed that people would get better and better jobs as time went on. So they gave mortgages with small down payments and assumed that the homeowners would get higher and higher wages or salaries so that they could make their payments of interest and principal of the loan. This bank behavior worked fairly well as long as the economy kept rising, so that people received more and more income. As soon as income started to stagnate in 2006 and to fall in the recession, the subprime loans could not be paid back. People lost their homes. Without these payments, banks and other home mortgage lenders got weaker and weaker, till many went bankrupt (as discussed in Chapter 8).

In the second quarter of 2008, the economy did a little better and the recession took a breather. So the rate of decline of housing construction slowed, but was still well over 10 percent a year. After that, as the economy got much worse, the decline of housing construction was at 24 percent a year in the fourth quarter of 2008.

In brief, housing construction and the general business cycle interact. In this case, housing construction led the downward economic spiral. Its bad mortgage loans hurt the financial system, which hurt the rest of the economy. When the economy did a little better in the first half of 2008, it caused housing to decline a little slower. When the rest of the economy declined faster in the last half of 2008, so did housing construction.

## Housing Prices in the Great Recession, 2007 to 2009

The extreme rise in housing prices from 1970 to 2001 was an important part of the extraordinary boom in housing. Their subsequent rapid decline in 2008 and 2009 was an important part of the extraordinary crash in the housing market.

Figure 6.6 reveals how housing prices acted in the first five quarters of the Great Recession. Figure 6.6, the only figure that goes into 2009, tells a very clear story about housing prices. Housing prices continued to extend the bubble by a tiny bit even in the last quarter of 2007, when the Great Recession officially began. Then the bubble started to break in the beginning of 2008.

Figure 6.6    **Housing Prices in the Crisis, 2007.4–2009.1**

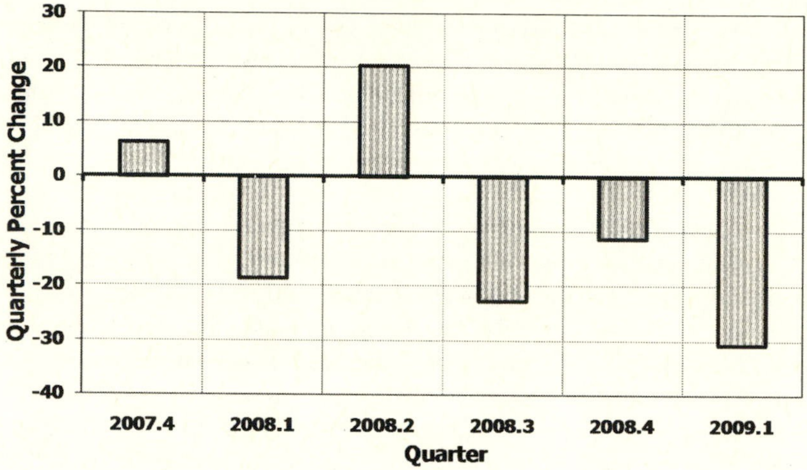

*Source:* U.S. Census Bureau (www.census.gov).
*Note:* Average sales price of houses sold, percent change, quarter to quarter, in annual rates, 2007.4 to 2009.1, in current dollars, at annual rates.

When GDP recovered a little in the second quarter of 2008, housing prices breathed their last gasp upward. In the next three quarters of the severe recession, housing prices declined rapidly. By the fourth quarter of 2008, housing prices declined at an annual rate of 30 percent! So the great boom in housing was followed by the crash in housing.

For the entire period from the 1970s to 2007, the growth of real wages and salaries has been sluggish to nonexistent. This meant that it was harder and harder for the average American to buy a home because housing prices continued to rise faster than most other prices.

So what fueled the great housing boom? Obviously, the answer is increasing credit in the form of mortgages. This was a major part of the story of the credit balloon, to be told in Chapter 8.

**Clues to Remember**

What can be concluded about housing crises? Usually, before there is a crisis, there is first a long period in which house construction increases rapidly. The price of housing soars to the sky. This period results in a housing price bubble, called a bubble because it goes beyond the means of most homebuyers. The bubble is sustained only by giving credit to millions of people whose income is insufficient to cover their mortgage payments.

Eventually, this bubble collapses and millions of people lose their homes. In 2007, the housing crisis helped turn a weak economy with many problems into a depressed economy. The housing crisis harmed consumer spending through the wealth effect because people felt they had less wealth and therefore spent less on consumer goods and services. The housing crisis also harmed the financial system through risky mortgages that went bad.

When such a crisis in housing coincides with a general business contraction, it is one of the factors that may turn a mild recession into a deep or Great Recession. Two other important factors may also help change a recession into a Great Recession. These are a financial crisis and a similar downturn in the rest of the world.

In times when the rest of the U.S. economy was healthy, the financial system strong, and the rest of the world in good shape, a decline in housing prices did not lead to a Great Recession. Unfortunately, in 1929 and again in 2008, these three factors were all negative.

**Suggested Reading**

An excellent article that explains the housing crisis is Robert Pollin's "The Housing Bubble and Financial Deregulation: Isn't Enough Enough?" *New Labor Forum* 17, no. 2 (2008a): 118–121.

**Appendix: Housing Starts**

One more bit of data strongly reinforces the picture painted in this chapter. The economic series called "housing starts" records the very beginning of construction. Thus, it affords a first sign of an upturn or downturn in housing. Figure 6.7 reveals the course of housing starts in both the previous five cycles and the present cycle.

There are important similarities as well as a startling difference between the two cycle patterns. In the average expansion of the five cycles from 1970 to 2001, housing starts rose until the middle of the business expansion, and then fell moderately for the rest of the expansion. In the average recession of the five cycles, housing starts fell a little, and then recovered, so they were fairly flat for the whole recession.

In the Bush expansion of 2001 to 2007, the pattern seemed much the same. Housing starts rose to the middle of the expansion, and then fell at a medium rate for the rest of the expansion. But there the similarities end. Housing starts fell fast and far in the Great Recession of 2007 to 2008—and they are still falling in 2009. So housing starts fully reflect the long-run balloon in housing and the present crash.

Figure 6.7  **Housing Starts by Cycle, 1970–2001 and 2001–2008**

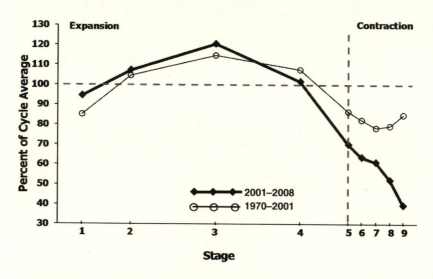

*Source:* U.S. Census Bureau (www.census.gov).
*Note:* Housing starts are new privately owned housing units started. Latest cycle, 2001.4 to 2008.4, and average of five cycles, 1970.4 to 2001.4, in thousands of housing units, seasonally adjusted at annual rates, monthly data aggregated to quarterly data.

# 7

# Investment and Profit

This chapter looks at structural change in the investment sector, and then focuses on the cyclical behavior of investment and profit.

**Secular Changes in Investment**

Long ago in the early nineteenth century, all money for investment came from individual saving. In the last few decades, however, the percentage of personal income going to saving has steadily declined until it has often been zero or negative. Negative personal saving for the whole country means that the average person is going into debt.

Then, for a long time, a great deal of aggregate saving in America was done by corporations that reinvested it as needed. There is still some investment out of retained profits, but most investment is now from borrowed money. Much of that money is borrowed from abroad, including developing countries such as China. The decade-long increased use of credit by corporations was a key part of the problems leading to the crisis of 2008.

**A Story About Investment and Profit**

In the jungle, the elephant is the largest creature and has enormous strength, but it usually moves pretty slowly. The cheetah is much smaller, but it moves like the wind.

Consumer spending is similar to the elephant. It moves very slowly, but it is by far the largest component of the GDP. It must, therefore, play an important role in the business cycle. For example, when the growth of consumer spending slows down to a very low level in the last part of an expansion, the slower growth of consumption has a negative effect on

Table 7.1

**Consumption and Investment** (in percent)

|  | Expansion<br>Stage 5 minus Stage 1 | Contraction<br>Stage 9 minus Stage 5 |
|---|---|---|
| Consumption | 19.93 | 0.70 |
| Nonresidential | 36.79 | −8.76 |

*Source:* Bureau of Economic Analysis, Department of Commerce (www.bea.gov).
*Note:* Consumption is real personal consumption expenditures (aggregate consumer spending). Investment is real nonresidential private domestic investment. Both are average of five cycles, 1970 to 2001, in billions of chained 2000 dollars, seasonally adjusted. Expansion is percent change from initial trough to cycle peak. Contraction is percent change from cycle peak to final trough.

corporate profit. The lower profit reduces expectations and creates a gloomy atmosphere for investment decisions. Therefore, it tends to reduce the investment in consumer goods and services.

Investment spending is more like the cheetah. It is not a large percentage of GDP, but it does move very fast. It runs rapidly up the hill during an expansion. Then it runs rapidly down the hill during a contraction. Investment moves so fast because investors' businesses try to react immediately to new conditions, and they often over-react. When there is an economic recovery, corporations and individuals move to invest as swiftly as possible. When corporations and rich individuals see an economic downturn, they rush to get their money out of the system as swiftly as possible. In a recession, corporations fire thousands of employees every day. The data on consumer spending and investment in the ups and downs of the business cycle are presented in Table 7.1. The table shows that in the average expansion of the five cycles from 1970 to 2001, consumer spending rose but it rose fairly slowly. Investment, on the other hand, rose very rapidly.

In the average contraction of the five cycles from 1970 to 2001, consumption fell a little at the beginning of the recession, then recovered, and was up very, very slightly at the end. People beg, borrow, and steal to keep up their level of consumption in a recession, with a heavy emphasis on borrowing. Finally, the table shows that the amount of investment in the economy fell drastically in each recession. Even though the average decline of GDP was fairly small, the table shows the rapid decline of investment in the recession.

Understanding investment is the key to understanding the roller coaster economy. Investment spending is one of the components of aggregate spending, along with consumption and government and net exports. Chapters 5 and 6 discussed at length spending for consumer goods and services, as well as for housing. These two chapters showed that consumption and housing are strongly affected by employee income. They are also strongly affected by credit. Chapter 7 will show that investment fluctuates very much over the business cycle and is most strongly affected by expectations of profit.

## Decision to Invest

The word "investment," as used by economists, always means the purchase by business of new buildings and equipment, which allows business to expand the amount of goods and services produced. This is very different from the common usage of "investment" to include personal investment in a car, a house, a piece of land, or a share of stock. These actions have no direct effect on the expansion of the productive base of the economy. If one person sells stock to another, it is just a change of ownership. Only if a corporation issues new stock and uses the money to buy equipment or buildings or both is there aggregate investment in the economy.

The decision by a corporation to invest requires two things. One is the funds necessary to make the investment. The other is the motivation to invest, based on expectations of profit.

Corporations have three sources of funds for investment in modern American capitalism. First, business used to get almost all its funds from the personal saving of individuals. Chapter 5 showed that personal saving in the United States had dropped to a little below zero and is now a little above zero. The saving of some rich individuals is balanced by the new debts of a large part of the poor and the middle-income employees. So personal saving is no longer an important source of business investment for the economy as a whole.

Second, the corporation retains some profit. It pays some profit out as dividends to stockholders, but it keeps some for further investment. This is an important source of corporate investment.

Corporations get a small amount of money for new investment from individual savers. Corporations get a larger sum of money for investment from their own retained earnings. The third source of corporate funds for investment is borrowing from financial institutions. Credit is now the most important source of investment funds. When credit dries up, there is little or no new investment. The use of corporate credit for investment purposes will be discussed in the next chapter.

## Investment for Expansion or for Speculation?

Business investment is defined as the buildings and equipment that increase the ability to produce more goods and services. Specifically, it means purchase of buildings and equipment.

A corporation may instead choose not to invest in productive facilities, but rather to make speculative investments. A mere change in who holds an asset, such as one person buying stock from another, does not produce anything. Speculative investment includes buying land with the intention of waiting until it rises in value. Also, a corporation may "invest" in buying back large amounts of its own stock because it expects the stock to rise in value. Such purchases of assets for speculative reasons do not increase aggregate investment because they do not purchase any new equipment or buildings.

Why do individuals and corporations make speculative purchases of land or stock or just hold cash in the bank rather than making productive investments? People and corporations invest to make a profit. If they see that they can make a profit down the road by installing new equipment or new buildings, then they will do that. If they do not expect to make a profit from productive investment in the economy, then they will use their funds for speculation or hold cash for emergencies.

Both individuals and corporations want certainty when they invest. The U.S. economy, however, frequently generates uncertainty. When things look uncertain for the future, corporations do not put money into productive investments. They worry that the productive investment may take several years to pay a profit or may never produce a profit at all.

### Investment Based on the Profit Motive

Business owners who contemplate the purchase of new buildings or equipment will not decide to make the purchase unless the profit they expect to receive from this investment is greater than the purchase price of the buildings and equipment. Profit is exceedingly important in determining the level of investment and employment in the U.S. economy.

Indeed, the prime motivation for investment in a capitalist economy is the expectation of future profit on the new investment. Yet, because future profit cannot be known with certainty, it is mainly on past profit that business people base their expectations. Accordingly, high or rising profit will lead to optimistic expectations and a rise in new investment.

Profit is the motive for investment and the source of some investment funds. There is, therefore, a close relationship between investment decisions and profit. In making a decision on whether to invest at a particular time, business people seem most heavily influenced by the movements of profit in the previous few quarters, which are the basis for expectations of future profit. (Statistical tests indicating the close relationship of investment and profit are discussed in Sherman 1991.)

## Psychological Attitudes on Investment

In the last quarter of 2008, there was extreme pessimism about the economy. Very few individuals wanted to buy stock, while very few corporations wanted to invest in expansions of their business. This pessimism was the basic cause of the lack of investment.

What was the cause of the pessimism? There had already been a year of the Great Recession and falling corporate profits. There was now a financial crisis and a precipitous fall in corporate profits. Therefore, the objective facts of profit movements caused the pessimism. In fact, all economic pessimism or optimism has some objective economic cause.

So economic decisions by the aggregate of all investors can be traced back to profit movements. The pessimism or optimism that follows in the wake of profit changes does enormously magnify and exaggerate the profit movements. So instead of a mild decline of investment, there may be a crash. Instead of a mild expansion of investment, there may be a boom, with a balloon effect far beyond the objective movements of profit.

## Investment and Profit in Five Cycles, 1970 to 2001

Corporate profit was one source of investment funds and was the incentive for investment in the five cycles from 1970 to 2001, as it has been in all U.S. cycles. Figure 7.1 illustrates the relationship between investment and profit at every stage of the cycle.

This figure is named simply "Investment and Profit," but those terms must be defined in order to clarify the topic. Profit means corporate profit, adjusted for inflation. Investment means nonresidential investment, adjusted for inflation. The previous chapter told the story of housing construction, which is officially called residential investment. So investment, officially called nonresidential investment, means all equipment and buildings used for expanding the production of the economy.

In Figure 7.1, investment rises rapidly for most of the expansion, and then rises more slowly toward the peak of the expansion. Why does it behave that way? Examining profit gives the answer.

Profit at first rises even more rapidly than investment. Investment follows profit as a cat follows a mouse. In the last half of expansion, profit moves upward more and more slowly. Then, profit actually declines in the last stage of the expansion.

Investment follows profit with a time lag. So investment keeps rising more and more slowly. When profit falls in the last stage of expansion, it causes investment to fall after the peak in the beginning of the recession.

Figure 7.1 **Investment and Profit by Cycle, 1970–2001**

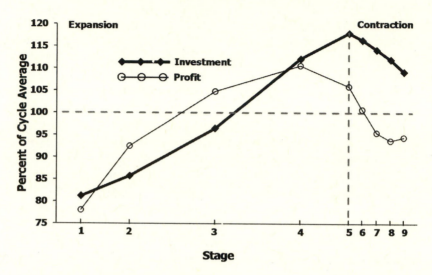

*Source:* Bureau of Economic Analysis, Department of Commerce (www.bea.gov).
   *Note:* Investment is real nonresidential private domestic investment. Profit is real corporate profit before taxes. Both series are the average of five cycles, 1970.4 to 2001.4, in
billions of chained 2000 dollars, seasonally adjusted quarterly data, at annual rates.

The fall of profit causes the fall of investment—and that signals the beginning of the recession.

During the recession phase of these five cycles, profit fell to the trough.
The decline of profit pulled down investment like an anchor tied to a man,
pulling him down under the water.

The investment decline causes the recession for two reasons. First, when
investment declines, it means immediately that fewer employees are needed
to design and build equipment and to build the buildings needed for the equipment. Second, it means that no new employees are being hired, so every new
person on the labor market becomes unemployed.

As unemployment rises for these two reasons, existing enterprises cannot
sell all the goods and services that they produce. Then those enterprises cut
back on production, firing more employees. The income of the unemployed
goes from a regular wage or salary to the small amount of unemployment
compensation provided by the government. With less income, there is less
buying power. The lower spending leads to less profit, which leads to less
investment. This is the vicious circle of a recession or a depression.

The decline in investment continues throughout the recession. Chapter 5
explained the reasons that consumer spending falls much less than the total

amount of goods and services produced. Chapters 8 and 10 show that interest costs and raw material costs both decline far faster than the gross product. The summary in Chapter 11 will show that in every recession, aggregate revenues usually fall much slower than aggregate costs. Therefore, aggregate profit bottoms out and expectations become more optimistic. The optimistic expectations lead to the beginning of a new investment recovery. This was the case in each of the five recessions from 1970 through 2001, each leading to a new recovery.

Investment closely follows the movements of profit for the reasons given earlier, but investment follows with a time lag. Why is there a time lag? Suppose conditions change and the economy looks more profitable. It takes some time before the business knows about the general economic improvement because it takes information a while to be recorded and read. Even a single large business takes some time to know just how it has performed in the last month.

Second, after learning that the outlook for profit is improving, the business must figure out exactly what new facilities it wants to build or what equipment it wants to buy. If a technological decision is needed, the owners must consult with experts.

Third, the business must usually borrow money from a financial institution. That process takes time.

Fourth, any major building requires government permits, which also take time.

Finally, a building is not built in a minute, so the actual investment is paid out slowly to a contractor over time.

## What Determines Profit?

This chapter has furnished a new, very powerful clue to the business cycle. It is the fact that the economy is controlled by investment, which is the only way that the economy expands. That investment is based on the outlook for profit making. Profit is the hero of the expansion and the villain of the recession. More precisely, the normal behavior of business profit in each recovery causes a more or less energetic expansion. When profit declines in the last stage of expansion, investment declines one stage later at the cycle peak. In the recession, profit declines and causes investment to decline further. Finally, toward the end of the recession, profit shows signs of recovery. This causes investment to start rising a stage later at the final cycle trough.

Now, by discovering all the clues to the behavior of profit, the circle is closed.

In making a profit, the capitalist owners of American corporations perform three operations. First, they use their money to buy what is needed for production. They buy physical capital goods, such as machinery and raw materials. They also buy labor—that is, the contractual right to use employees' power to labor for so many hours a day. Second, corporations use the capital and labor in a production process that must produce commodities with higher revenue than the cost of the capital and labor that went into them. Third, they sell the new commodities for money. Profit shows up here because the corporations sell the commodities for more money than they used originally in buying the capital and labor.

Obstacles to profit can arise within the United States in the private sector if (1) the cost of labor power and capital goods rises, (2) there is a decline in the productivity of the production process, or (3) there is insufficient demand for the commodities that have been produced. An economic crisis comes whenever profit is squeezed lower by both a slower rise of revenue and higher costs.

Some writers emphasize that profit is squeezed at the end of expansion by rising costs. Other writers emphasize that profit is squeezed at the end of expansion by inadequate demand. This book shows that profit is squeezed from both sides at once.

At the end of every expansion, profit is reduced both by stagnant demand for goods and services, and by rising costs of production. Profit is squeezed like a nut in a nutcracker at the end of expansion, causing a recession or depression. Profit expands again as the nutcracker loosens at the end of the contraction, opening the way to recovery.

## Summary of Investment and Profit in the Previous Five Cycles

Investment spending swings rather violently up and down, fluctuating far more than consumer spending. The strong swings of investment dominate the economy and are the immediate cause of all economic ups and downs.

The behavior of investment follows with a time lag after profit, which itself moves up and down rapidly. Thus, when profit declines in the last stage of expansion, investment declines because profit declines, but with a time lag. In the last stage of contraction, the expectation of profit (and sometime profit itself) rises, causing investment to rise at the beginning of the next expansion.

## The Expansion, 2001 to 2007

The above sections have stated the usual behavior of profit and investment in the last five recessions. The recent Bush expansion and the Great Recession of 2007 to 2009 were similar in some basic respects, but the Great Recession

Figure 7.2 **Investment and Profit by Year, 2001–2007**

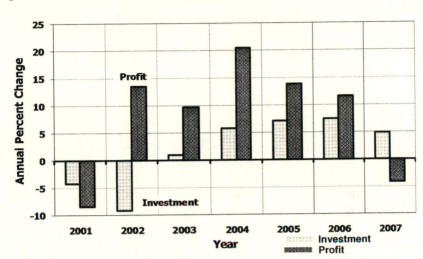

*Source:* Bureau of Economic Analysis, Department of Commerce (www.bea.gov).
*Note:* Investment is real nonresidential private domestic investment. Profit is real corporate profit before taxes. Both series are percent change, year to year, 2001 to 2007, in billions of chained 2000 dollars, annual data.

was more violent than any other postwar recession. The incredible growth of profits in the Bush expansion and the equally incredible fall of profit in the Great Recession were also far more violent than anything in the past five cycles.

The expansion of profit and investment from 2001 through 2007 is charted in Figure 7.2. In this figure, investment means nonresidential investment. Profit means corporate profit. The effect of inflation is corrected by deflating both variables, so the movements are in real terms.

Figure 7.2 shows that profit and investment fell in the recession of 2001— not a big surprise. Then profit and investment rose and picked up speed until the middle of the expansion in 2004. Over the course of the expansion, corporate profits skyrocketed, increasing 11 percent a year, after adjusting for inflation. This rate of growth of profits was far higher than the 8 percent average in other expansions from World War II to 2001. After correcting for inflation, wages and salaries did far less well. They grew just 1.8 percent a year during this expansion, less than half the 3.8 percent rate during the average expansion from World War II to 2001.

In the last half of the expansion, profits did grow more slowly. Yet "slow" here means over 10 percent growth, starting from a record-high level. Only in the last half of 2007 did profit begin to fall, just one quarter before the Great Recession began. This profit peak and decline forecast the cycle peak and the decline of investment and GDP.

Since investment rose slowly over much of the expansion, the Bush expansion was weaker in growth than the average of the previous five cycles.

As in the previous five cycles, the movement of investment followed profit, but with the usual time lag and at a much lower growth rate. Thus, investment continued to rise in 2007 even after profit was falling. The growth of investment, however, was slower and slower toward the peak. Only in 2008, when the Great Recession deepened and the financial crisis was in full swing, did investment fall. The next section will show that the decline was extraordinarily rapid.

**The Great Recession, 2007 to 2009**

The expansion of 2001 to 2007 was somewhat weaker than average in terms of the increase of investment. It was even weaker in terms of the growth of wages and salaries. The sluggish growth of employee income slowed down the growth of consumer spending. The slowing of consumption growth was one of the several causes leading to a decline of profit and ultimately a Great Recession.

One other reason for the decline in profit was the end of the housing bubble, as detailed in Chapter 6. The fall in house prices made credit far harder for homeowners to obtain. Chapters 8 through 10 will show that the consumption gap and the housing crisis were aided and abetted by a credit crisis, by the slowing of government spending, and by a more negative trade balance with the rest of the world.

The behavior of corporate profit and investment during the Great Recession is shown in real terms in Figure 7.3, revealing that corporate profit fell from the beginnings of the Great Recession. In the first four quarters of the Great Recession, corporate profit fell 5 to 10 percent a quarter (at annual rates, as in all of these data). Then, in the fourth quarter of 2008, there was a financial panic.

During the financial crisis in the fourth quarter of 2008, investment fell at an annual rate of 30 percent, while corporate profits fell at the extraordinary annual rate of 50 percent. The investment and profit data are both corrected for inflation, so these numbers are in real terms. The change from very rapid profit growth to very rapid profit decline in such a short period is breathtaking.

That drop signaled the beginning of the deepest part of the Great Recession and the financial crisis—though it is unknown at the time of this writing how long it will last.

Figure 7.3 **Investment and Profit in the Crisis, 2007.4–2008.4**

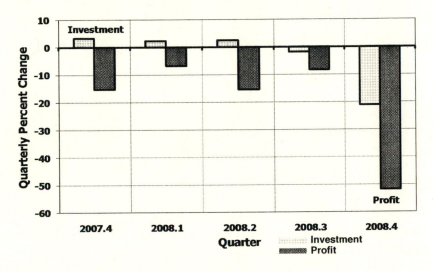

*Source:* Bureau of Economic Analysis, Department of Commerce (www.bea.gov).
*Note:* Investment is real nonresidential private domestic investment. Profit is real corporate profit before taxes. Both series are percent change, quarter to quarter, 2007.4 to 2008.4, in billions of chained 2000 dollars, seasonally adjusted quarterly data, at annual rates.

Throughout this serious recession, investment followed profit downward, but with a time lag. At first, investment moved very little. Then the effect of falling profit finally caught up with the investment process. In the third quarter of 2008, the amount of investment fell a little. Finally, in the fourth quarter of 2008, investment fell over a cliff and started a rapid descent down into a Great Recession and a full-fledged financial crisis.

**Clues to Remember**

This chapter has shown that investment plays a vital role in the business cycle because it rises rapidly in most of the expansion and falls rapidly in most of a recession or depression. Its main sources of funds are corporate profit and credit. The sole incentive for corporate investment is the prospect of corporate profit. Thus investment follows profit. There is a time lag based on the time it takes for businesses to gather information, make their calculations and plans, and then execute them.

91

## The Hunt for Clues Continues

Although this chapter has shown how profit shapes investment, it has not explained what determines profit in any detail. Only a few clues were given as to the reasons for the rise and fall of profit. It was said that profit is determined by corporate revenue and corporate costs.

The discussion of costs was limited to the real economy, leaving aside the use of credit until Chapter 8. Thus Chapter 7 discussed the fact that employee income rises more slowly than national output or national income in every expansion, but did not consider the credit that employees get to help maintain their consumption levels. The chapter did examine the slowing of consumption in the last expansion, but has not yet clarified the role of credit, leaving that to Chapter 8.

Housing was considered, but without an explicit discussion of mortgage credit, to be found in Chapter 8. Chapter 7 related investment to corporate profit, but did not discuss corporate credit, interest rates, and the stock market, all to be found in the next chapter.

The sources of consumer and investment spending were discussed, but not the great elephant of government spending, which will be discussed along with taxes in Chapter 9.

Finally, the discussion of demand was limited to the domestic economy. Spending must be considered from a global economic view. Thus Chapter 10 includes a discussion of imports and exports, international investment, and international finance.

The clues will all be brought together to solve the mystery of profit swings and the roller coaster behavior of boom and bust in Chapter 11.

# The Credit Balloon and the Financial Crisis

Chapter 8 examines consumer and corporate credit, plus the financial crisis. It has an appendix on the stock market, an appendix on interest rates, and an appendix on how Janet predicted the stock market.

**Financial Crises and Structural Change**

To understand the financial crisis of 2008 to 2009, readers must understand the Federal Reserve System, which is supposed to regulate finance. There was a bad financial crisis in 1907, which led to the birth of the Federal Reserve.

The Federal Reserve System was begun in 1912. It was supposed to prevent financial crises by requiring banks to keep minimum necessary reserves and by lending to banks as a last resort to save them.

In the Great Depression of the 1930s, however, the Federal Reserve failed to preserve the banks. They were all closed, and then slowly reopened with many new regulations and safeguards.

By the 1960s, people began to forget the terrible financial crisis of the 1930s. Since the 1960s, there has been a broad movement of all kinds of conservatives to end as many regulations as possible. By 2007, most financial regulations were gone. It was explained that competition made the system self-regulating, so no regulations were needed. Even the few remaining regulations were evaded by the financial corporations to a remarkable degree. Each new president, from President Reagan through President George W. Bush, got rid of more regulations.

## Consumer Credit, 1970 to 2001

When consumers borrow money from a financial agency, they obtain a certain amount of credit. Consumer credit grew enormously from 1970 to 2001. In fact, Figure 8.1 shows nothing but growth in the average cycle from 1970 to 2001. Credit grows in the expansion. Credit also grows in the recession, but at a slightly slower rate.

Why did consumer credit rise so rapidly? Chapter 4 showed that the real income of the average employee grew very little in that period. Just to keep up with family needs, most Americans felt pressure to get more and more credit.

The really interesting question is whether the ratio of debt to an average person's income rose or fell. If debt rose by $1 trillion in some period, it might be nothing to worry about if income rose by $10 trillion. A rise of $1 trillion would be catastrophic if income rose by only $1 billion. What actually happened in this long period? In the 1970 to 1975 cycle, the ratio of consumer debt to national income was 64 percent on the average. This means that the debt owed by the average person was almost two-thirds of income in an average year. That is a lot of debt burden. By 2001, people owed an amount equal to their yearly income. In fact, the average person had to pay fourteen cents of every dollar earned for interest payments.

The amount of credit kept growing regardless of the cycle of expansion and recession. It just grew a little faster in expansions than in recessions. This was not a cyclical problem, just the long-run growth of a credit bubble of amazing proportions.

In fact, as long as people could get more credit it merely helped the expansion continue. It was only when, in 2008, people lost their jobs and banks no longer extended more credit that the situation became a disaster. The details of the disaster are discussed below in the sections on the expansion of 2001 to 2007 and the Great Recession.

## Consumer Credit in the Expansion, 2001 to 2007

Consumer credit continued its long rise in the expansion of 2001 to 2007. This is shown in Figure 8.2, which reveals that the growth of credit jumped to a high point in the recession of 2001. The reason was that people needed emergency credit in the hard times.

In the expansion that followed from 2002 to 2007, outstanding credit rose steadily by an average of 5 percent a year, though the rate of increase slowly declined. This rise helped the expansion continue. It helped people survive as long as they could get more credit.

Why was this process headed for disaster? The problem was that the vast

Figure 8.1   **Consumer Credit by Cycle, 1970–2001**

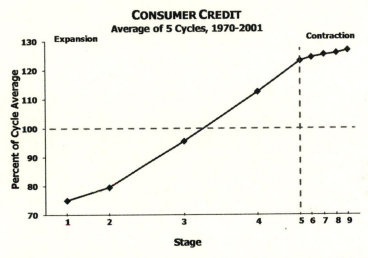

*Source:* Federal Reserve Board of Governors, table G.19, series G19/CCOUT/ DTCTL.M (www.federalreserve.gov).

*Note:* Consumer credit means consumer credit outstanding, the total consumer credit owned and securitized. Average of five cycles, 1970.4 to 2001.4, in billions of current dollars, seasonally adjusted monthly data, aggregated to quarterly data.

increase of credit over such a long time made the economy exceedingly fragile. It became a bubble ready to burst with any sudden pinprick. When the Great Recession struck, people could not maintain the payments to their banks for loans and to corporations for things they had bought.

**Consumer Credit in the Great Recession, 2007 to 2009**

The Great Recession began in the fourth quarter of 2007. The progress of consumer credit in the Great Recession is shown quarter by quarter until the end of 2008 in Figure 8.3.

Consumer credit continued to rise at about the same rate in the first three quarters of the Great Recession. Then its rate of growth diminished. Finally, in the fourth quarter of 2008, the bottom of the credit market dropped out. A disaster occurred. For the first time in many years, consumer credit actually declined by a significant amount. But because of mounting job losses, household incomes were falling nearly as quickly.

The decline of consumer incomes and the decline of consumer debt came as a vast surprise to most people. When retailers have grown accustomed to

Figure 8.2  **Consumer Credit by Year, 2001–2007**

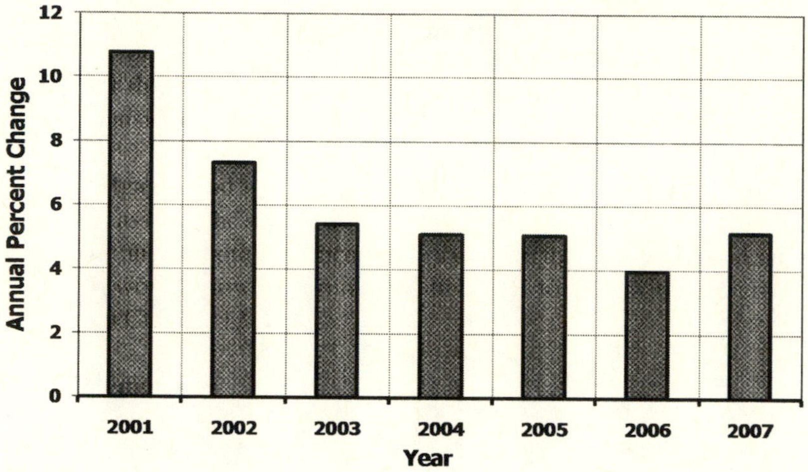

*Source:* Federal Reserve Board of Governors, table G.19, series G19/CCOUT/ DTCTL.M (www.federalreserve.gov).

*Note:* Consumer credit means consumer credit outstanding, the total consumer credit owned and securitized. Percent change, year to year, 2001 to 2007, in billions of current dollars, seasonally adjusted monthly data, aggregated to annual data.

expanding sales every quarter, they plan their inventories on that basis. They order what they expect to need from manufacturers. When sales fall off because of lack of credit, they suddenly find they have relatively large inventories of goods that cannot be sold at the current price. Their profit is reduced by fewer sales and by lower prices.

As the retailers cut back their orders, manufacturers cut back their production and fire large numbers of employees. The manufacturing corporations cannot pay back their own loans from banks. At the same time, the consumers cannot pay back their loans to banks. Every actor in the economic drama is hurt. There is a vicious spiral downward of less buying power, fewer purchases, less production, more unemployment, and still fewer loans to individuals.

**Corporate Credit in the Five Cycles, 1970 to 2001**

There was no cyclical pattern in corporate credit from 1970 to 2001. Corporations kept borrowing more and more throughout the period from 1970 to 2007. The rate of growth was about the same in expansions and recessions. The corporate credit bubble grew and grew in an extraordinary manner from 1970 to 2001. This can be seen in Figure 8.4.

Figure 8.3 **Consumer Credit in the Crisis, 2007.4–2008.4**

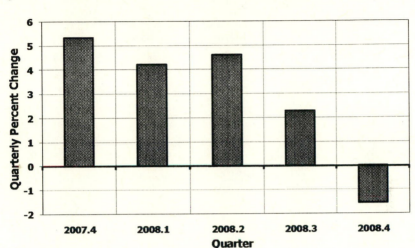

*Source:* Federal Reserve Board of Governors, table G.19, series G19/CCOUT/
DTCTL.M (www.federalreserve.gov).

*Note:* Consumer credit means consumer credit outstanding, the total consumer credit
owned and securitized. Percent change, quarter-to-quarter, 2007.4 to 2008.4, in billions
of current dollars, seasonally adjusted monthly data, aggregated to quarterly data, at
annual rates.

To understand corporate credit behavior, one must understand how corporations get the money to expand through new investment. Once upon a time,
much of the money for investment in a business came from the personal saving of its owners. Those times are long forgotten except in nostalgic movies.
In the 2001 to 2007 expansion, personal saving hovered around zero percent
of national income. Usually it was just above zero, but it was below zero in
some quarters. Below zero meant that the average person's debts grew faster
than the person's income.

If corporations did not get their investment money from personal saving,
where did they get it? For a time, much of it came from the corporation's own
profits. But by the 1970s, this source became far smaller than credit.

The largest corporations acquired high "leverage" and were proud of
that. Leverage meant that they had borrowed billions of dollars from other
people, and then used it to expand rapidly. By these means they made
amazing amounts of profit. Suppose the corporation's initial capital was
$1 billion, and it borrowed $10 billion more. Then, if prosperity continued
and the company made the average profit rate on all $11 billion, the rate of
total profit of its own $1 billion would be eleven times the average rate. So

Figure 8.4 **Corporate Credit by Cycle, 1970–2001**

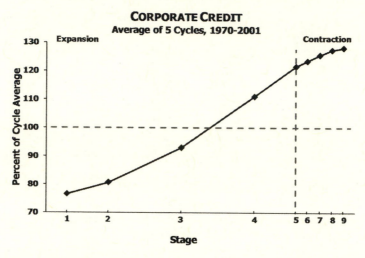

**CORPORATE CREDIT**
**Average of 5 Cycles, 1970-2001**

*Source:* Federal Reserve Board of Governors, table Z.1, series Z1/Z1/LA104104005.Q (www.federalreserve.gov).

*Note:* Corporate credit means nonfarm, nonfinancial corporate business credit marked instruments liability. Average of five cycles, 1970.4 to 2001.4, in billions of current dollars, seasonally adjusted quarterly data.

to make maximum profit, corporations just kept borrowing more and more. The bubble kept growing.

Is borrowing in an expansion always a bad thing? Obviously not in the short run. American corporations mainly used credit to expand their equipment and buildings. So the corporations benefited and the economy benefited by a longer expansion.

The problem is that the corporations became more vulnerable and fragile. They bet on rapid expansion of their sales. A small decline would mean that they could not repay their debt, could not pay the interest on the debt, and could not pay their employees or their suppliers. When the decline came in 2008, many corporations were quickly ruined.

**Corporate Credit in the Expansion, 2001 to 2007**

Figure 8.5 shows what happened to corporate credit in the expansion of 2001 to 2007. The graph of corporate credit is quite unusual. Corporate credit continued to grow moderately in the 2001 recession. Credit did not grow because corporations wanted to expand because there was no expansion. In the recession of 2001, many companies desperately needed credit to keep them

Figure 8.5 **Corporate Credit by Year, 2001–2007**

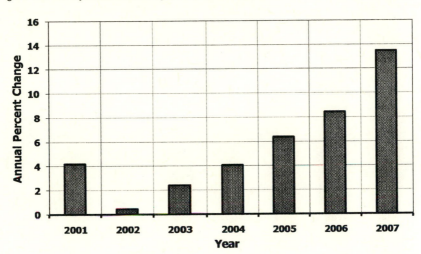

*Source:* Federal Reserve Board of Governors, table Z.1, series Z1/Z1/LA104104005.Q (www.federalreserve.gov).

*Note:* Corporate credit means nonfarm, nonfinancial corporate business credit marked instruments liability. Percent change, year to year, 2001 to 2007, in billions of current dollars, seasonally adjusted quarterly data, aggregated to annual data.

running in the mildly declining economy of the recession. They needed the new credit to pay back old loans, to pay employees, and to pay for supplies.

From 2002 to 2007, credit grew every year. Not only did credit grow, but also its rate of growth continued to rise. From less than 1 percent in 2002, when the expansion was extremely weak, the annual growth rate of corporate credit grew and grew to the boom rate of almost 14 percent in the peak year of 2007. Corporations continued to get higher profits from more leverage through more credit. This was a fragile bubble that was ready to burst.

## Corporate Credit in the Great Recession, 2007 to 2009

The graph of corporate credit in the Great Recession is striking. Its movement is diametrically opposite. This behavior is portrayed in Figure 8.6.

In the first four quarters of the recession, Figure 8.6 shows that corporate credit moved at a slower growth rate in every quarter. Corporations wanted to borrow more because their income had dropped. They did not have enough income to pay the interest and principal of their debts and also to pay employees and suppliers. Banks, however, were less and less willing to advance more credit as corporate profits looked worse and worse.

Figure 8.6 **Corporate Credit in the Crisis, 2007.4–2008.4**

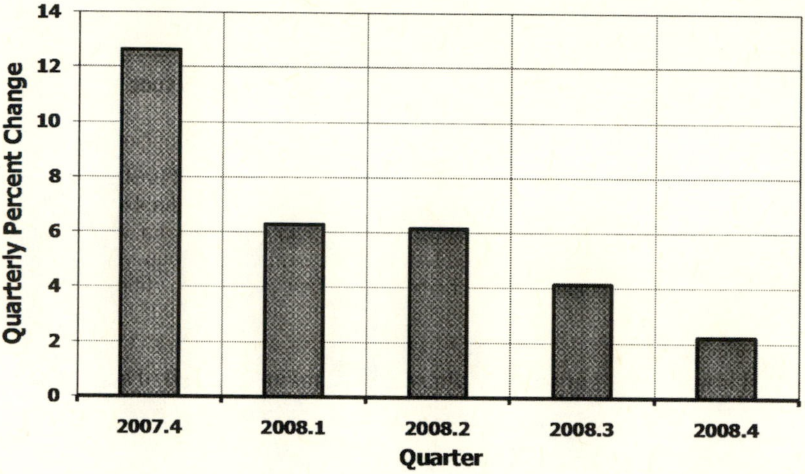

*Source:* Federal Reserve Board of Governors, table Z.1, series Z1/Z1/LA104104005.Q (www.federalreserve.gov).

*Note:* Corporate credit means nonfarm, nonfinancial corporate business credit marked instruments liability. Percent change, quarter to quarter, 2007.4 to 2008.4, in billions of current dollars, seasonally adjusted quarterly data, at annual rates.

In the fourth quarter of 2008, outstanding corporate credit rose only about 1 percent. Since corporate income was declining, but corporate credit was tiny, companies could no longer pay their employees, their suppliers, or their interest payments to the banks. Most corporations fired large numbers of employees. Many companies went bankrupt. The ceasing of payment to the banks was one of the causes of the financial crisis.

**The Financial Crisis**

Changes in economic structure set the stage for the financial crisis, while cyclical problems set it off. There were four main changes in the structure of the economy that led to the crisis. First, the long-run stagnation of real wages and salaries meant that the corporations could no longer take for granted continued growth in the demand for goods and services. Thus they could no longer count on growing income and consumer spending to solve all problems. Second, the dangerous and extraordinary growth of the credit bubble occurred.

Third, most financial regulations and safeguards had disappeared after several decades of work by their opponents. This meant that banks could and did make extremely risky loans to increase their short-run profits. Fourth, there was an extraordinary boom in housing that lasted almost four decades (with a few minor declines). This could be seen in the large increase of home prices over the period.

Then there were immediate cyclical problems. The first problem was that lack of consumer income had been solved by an enormous increase in consumer credit for forty years. The rapid growth of consumer credit postponed the recession, but its price was increased economic fragility. When employment and income fell in 2007 and 2008, consumers could no longer pay their debts to the industrial corporations, such as General Motors, or to the financial corporations, such as Bank of America. This severely weakened the financial system.

The second problem came from the huge bubble of corporate debt. As shown above, when corporate income declined in the severe recession, companies could not pay their bills or debts. Many went bankrupt. The effect on the financial system was powerful. The weakened or even bankrupt corporations could no longer supply a flow of money payments to the banks and other financial corporations (such as the immense insurance company, AIG).

As if the declining ability of consumers and corporations to pay the banks was not enough, the third problem came when the housing increase slowed and then turned down. The biggest single asset of the banks and other financial corporations was the mortgages they owned. The housing industry had expanded without stop for more than thirty-five years. Housing prices had risen all that time. The supply of credit to buy homes through mortgages had risen all that time.

Millions of people had mortgages. In many cases, it was clear that they would have trouble paying them on their existing income. The risk-taking attitude of the lenders and financial corporations was: Why the hell not give them large mortgages? The lenders assumed that employee income would slowly rise, so they could pay, though perhaps with difficulty. Moreover, the price of the house would continue to rise. Therefore, even if the employee/house-owner could not pay the mortgage, the house could be foreclosed. Foreclosure was considered safe by the lenders because the price of houses would continue to rise.

Thus, there were millions of risky mortgages. On top of this risk, the financial corporations evolved a scheme in which one sold mortgages to another, with each firm making a profit along the way. So one mortgage supported a pyramid of financial transactions all over the world. When the housing market went bad, big banks in Germany suffered as much as big banks in the United States.

And housing did go bad. As shown in Chapter 6, housing construction began to decline in 2006 and has continued to decline until now in 2009. Housing prices rose monstrously for almost forty years, but have declined more than one-third since 2007. This decline in housing, with hundreds of thousands of foreclosures amid falling price knocked out the supports from the flimsy palace of finance.

Finally, it must be emphasized that the financial crisis and panic greatly worsened the recession. Constriction of credit by the financial corporations meant that ordinary people could no longer get additional credit to support their normal way of life, especially when they lost their jobs. This meant less spending on goods and services, further harming the industrial corporations. The industrial corporations were caught between two fires. On the one hand, consumer support for goods and services sales was falling. On the other hand, banks and other lenders were refusing to make loans to get the corporations through the hard times. The financial crisis provided considerable justification for calling the severe downturn a Great Recession.

The mortgages and other bad loans of the financial system came to be called toxic assets. The spread of these toxic assets, along with the problems in consumer and corporate finance, led to a crisis in the whole financial sphere around the world. How governments attempted to deal with this crisis is discussed in Chapter 12.

**Clues to Remember**

First, consumer credit has played a major and increasing role in the purchase of consumer goods and services in every expansion. The increase of consumer credit has made each expansion more and more fragile.

Second, corporate credit has played a major and increasing role in the purchase of buildings and equipment for business in every expansion. The increase of corporate credit has made each expansion more and more fragile.

Third, the stock market has risen rapidly and become a tenuous balloon at the peak of each expansion, especially at the last two cycle peaks. When the stock market begins to fall, the wealth effect drags down consumer spending. The wealth effect includes the rising consumer optimism from a rising stock market, but also the reluctance of consumers to spend when their stock values decline.

Fourth, interest rates rise in every expansion, but they continue to rise a little further at the beginning of most recessions. In the 2007 to 2009 Great Recession, however, interest rates began falling as soon as the downturn in the economy commenced.

## Suggested Readings

The usual pattern of consumer credit in the business cycle is detailed in Howard J. Sherman's *The Business Cycle: Growth and Crisis Under Capitalism* (1991), and the patterns of recent years are discussed in Robert Pollin's *Contours of Descent: U.S. Economic Fractures and the Landscape of Global Austerity* (2004).

## Appendix 8.1: Interest Rates and the Roller Coaster

Figure 8.7 shows that interest rates followed a specific pattern in the economic expansion of the average cycle from 1970 to 2001. In the early recovery period after a recession, interest rates remain low and often decline. They do that because people and corporations remember the last recession and are afraid to borrow a lot of money. In addition to the lack of demand for loans, interest rates are often held down by the Federal Reserve System in order to stimulate the economy to a speedier recovery.

In most of the following expansions up until the peak, interest rates rise rapidly. The reason is the strong borrowing by consumers and corporations that was discussed in this chapter. The Federal Reserve also allows interest rates to rise because it believes that high interest rates might prevent the economy from rising so fast that it will create inflation.

When a mild recession begins, interest rates usually go higher for a while. The reason is that both consumers and corporations are desperate to get more credit to meet the unexpected problems of the recession, as shown in this chapter.

Finally, as the recession continues, the interest rate declines. The main reason is that there is less demand for loans because of the pessimism of consumers about jobs and the pessimism of corporations about making profits. The Federal Reserve also tries to keep interest rates low in order to stimulate business.

It will be seen below that the present expansion followed the usual pattern, but interest rates in the Great Recession did not follow the usual pattern in some respects.

Do higher interest rates tend to stifle the economy? Interest payments are a part of the cost of doing business; so higher interest rates do have some negative effect on business profits and investment. But interest payments are a small part of business costs, so the effect of higher interest rates only adds to the problems already there. High interest rates do not have much direct effect on consumer spending, except in housing and automobile sales. The reason is that loans are a big part of the sales process in those two areas.

Figure 8.7 **Prime Rate of Interest by Cycle, 1970–2001**

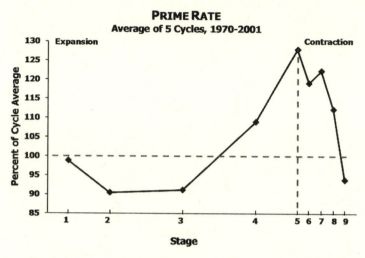

**PRIME RATE**
**Average of 5 Cycles, 1970-2001**

*Source:* Federal Reserve Board of Governors, table H.15, series H15/H15/RIFSPBLP _N.M (www.federalreserve.gov).

*Note:* Prime rate is the average majority prime rate charged by banks on short-term loans to business quoted on an investment basis. Average of five cycles, 1970.4 to 2001.4, in percent, monthly data aggregated to quarterly data.

Do lower interest rates help stimulate the economy? Since interest payments are a small part of the costs of most businesses, lowering them is helpful, but not very important in itself. If a corporation can borrow money at a low interest rate, it still will not do so unless it sees a profitable market for its goods. In a deep recession or depression, lower interest rates do no good because other things are far more important for profit.

### Interest Rates in the Expansion, 2001 to 2007

The interest rate in the Bush years is explored in a graph of the expansion of 2001 to 2007. Figure 8.8 uses the prime rate as a representative of the many different interest rates that exist.

Like most interest rates, the prime rate tends to lag behind at each cycle turning point. Thus, Figure 8.8 shows that the prime rate continued to fall for two years after the expansion of 2001 began. The reason for the lag is that people were still feeling the effects of the 2001 recession, so they had little confidence in the future of the economy. Therefore, they were unwilling to borrow for the purpose of increasing their consumption. Corporations were similarly lacking confidence, so they also did not borrow large amounts.

Figure 8.8  **Prime Rate of Interest by Year, 2001–2007**

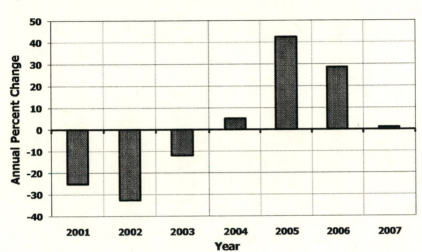

*Source:* Federal Reserve Board of Governors, table H.15, series H15/H15/RIFSPBLP
_N.M (www.federalreserve.gov).

*Note:* Prime rate is the average majority prime rate charged by banks on short-term
loans to business quoted on an investment basis. Percent change, year-to-year, 2001 to
2007, monthly data aggregated to annual data.

In the next three years of the expansion, 2004 to 2006, the prime rate, and
all other interest rates, increased. The prime rate increased in those years for
two reasons. First, there was a rise in confidence in the economy. So there was
borrowing to increase new investment or consumption. Second, the Federal
Reserve encouraged higher rates.

In the last year of the expansion, 2007, the prime rate remained almost
constant. By the end of that year, the Great Recession had begun.

### Interest Rates in the Great Recession

Figure 8.9 illustrates the fact that interest rate behavior in the Great Recession
did not follow the usual interest rate behavior in relatively mild recessions
in one respect.

In most recessions, interest rates lag at the cycle peak, continuing to rise
for some time after the peak. The Great Recession was strong enough that
the prime rate fell immediately in the fourth quarter of 2007 and continued to
fall in every quarter of 2008. In the dismal fourth quarter of 2008, the prime
rate fell over 50 percent in annual terms.

Figure 8.9    **Prime Rate of Interest in the Crisis, 2007.4–2008.4**

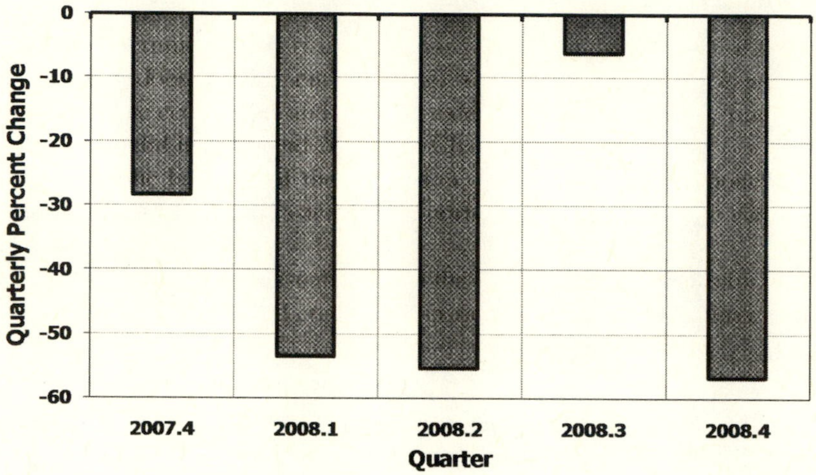

*Source:* Federal Reserve Board of Governors, table H.15, series H15/H15/RIFSPBLP _N.M (www.federalreserve.gov).

*Note:* Prime rate is the average majority prime rate charged by banks on short-term loans to business quoted on an investment basis. Percent change, quarter-to-quarter, 2007.4 to 2008.4, monthly data aggregated to quarterly data, at annual rates.

In addition to the pessimism that prevented borrowing, the Federal Reserve also did its best to reduce interest rates. Like so many other economic series, the prime rate did indeed fall a great deal. The theory of the Federal Reserve, echoing the dominant view in economics, was that a much lower interest rate would encourage consumers to borrow more money and spend it, thereby boosting the economy.

The Federal Reserve believed that lower interest rates would encourage corporations to invest. But at that time, neither consumers nor corporations had confidence in the economic system for the near future. Moreover, interest payments are just one factor in corporate profit. Even if interest payments go down, a corporation will still not borrow if there is no market for its goods and services.

**Appendix 8.2: Stock Market Boom and Crash**

Appendix 8.2 looks briefly at the average performance of the stock market in the five cycles from 1970 to 2001, and then looks carefully at stocks in the Bush expansion and the Great Recession.

### Stocks in Five Cycles, 1970 to 2001

In this period, the stock market generally rose with the economy and fell with the economy. Figure 8.10 shows its average behavior in the five cycles from 1970 to 2001.

This graph tells a story of the stock market that goes up and down with the cycle, but with one difference. It normally begins to decline a stage before the economy declines. It also tends to begin its decline before the economy reaches its peak. Finally, the stock market starts to recover before the aggregate economy recovers.

The first question is: why does the stock market normally go up and down with the economy? The answer is simple. The stock market follows corporate profit like a hunting dog follows a fox.

More intriguing is the question: why does the stock market usually lead the economy by six to eight months? Instead, one might expect that the stock market would follow the economy by six to nine months while it digests the news of where the economy is going.

What actually happens is that the stock market is very sensitive to profits. Corporate profits normally lead the economy by six to nine months. As shown in Chapter 7, profits decline because corporate revenue is rising more slowly than corporate costs. After profits decline, there is a time lag until investment and production start to decline for the reasons given in Chapter 7.

Since profits decline a stage before the cycle peaks, so does the stock market. Those who trade large amounts frequently in the stock market keep their eyes on the profits of each of the companies that trade their stocks in the market. As soon as they see a decline in profits in many corporations, they start to sell their stock.

Exactly the opposite happens in a recession. As the economic bottom is approached, some corporate profits rise. Then investment and production rise six to nine months later. As soon as a number of corporations start to make more profits, the big investors in the stock market know of it and begin to invest. Therefore, the stock market also begins to rise six to nine months in advance of the economy.

The above explains how the economy affects the stock market. What is the impact of the stock market on the economy? There is some, but not much. If a person buys a new stock issue from a corporation, and if the corporation uses the money from the investor to buy equipment and buildings, then there is investment and expansion. But the vast majority of stock market transactions are just transfers from one person to another, having no aggregate investment effect.

As explained in Chapter 5 on consumer spending, when stock prices fall,

Figure 8.10 **Stocks by Cycle, 1970–2001**

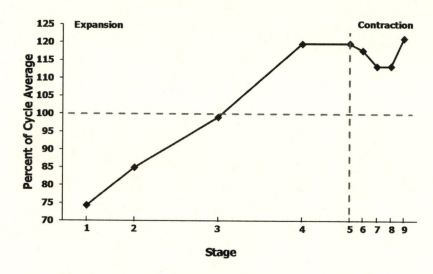

*Source:* Yahoo finance (www.yahoo.com).
*Note:* Stocks means Standard and Poor's 500 corporation stock index. Average of five cycles, 1970.4 to 2001.4, monthly data aggregated to quarterly data.

investors become less wealthy and cut back on consumption. If a rich person loses 1 million dollars in the stock market, they may reduce their consumption a little out of fear for their savings. If a poor person has all their savings in the stock market through a company saving fund, then the loss of half of it might be catastrophic. If the poor person is out of a job, they need their savings immediately, yet only half of it might still exist.

### The Stock Market in the Expansion, 2001 to 2007

Understanding the stock market is complicated because there are three components to its movements. First, it is influenced by day-to-day news of the economy, often over-reacting to this news.

Second, the stock market moves up and down in small cycles of its own. When the market goes up far and fast, speculators get worried and sell all of their stock, causing a decline for a month or two or three. When the stock market goes down too far and fast, speculators see a wonderful opportunity to buy a bargain, so they buy and cause the market to rise for a month or two or three.

Third, over the whole business cycle, stocks march along hand in hand with corporate profit. Both are leading indicators, meaning that they turn down

Figure 8.11 **Stocks by Year, 2001–2007**

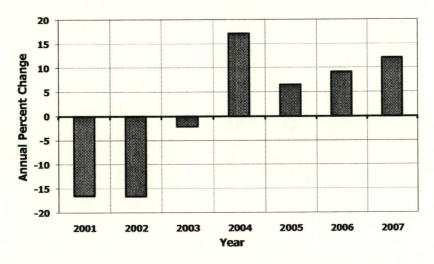

*Source:* Yahoo finance (www.yahoo.com).
*Note:* Stocks means Standard and Poor's 500 corporation stock index, percent change, year-to-year, 2001 to 2007, monthly data aggregated to annual data.

six to nine months before the cycle peaks, but they might also turn up six to nine months before the cycle trough. It is thus very easy to explain the stock market by hindsight, but almost impossible by foresight.

The behavior of the stock market in the expansion from 2001 to 2007 is given in Figure 8.11. It is possible to see in it how the stock market moves with profit (as shown in Chapter 7), but one cannot see the daily and monthly components of change.

The recession year of 2001 was very bad for the stock market, but so were the two following years. After the stock market recovered in 2003, the stock market grew for about four good years, averaging about 10 percent growth per year. This was a remarkable performance, but it only echoed the movement of corporate profits.

The three bad years in the stock market—2001, 2002, and early 2003 —represented the economic weakness of the expansion of 2001 to 2007. The four good years—2004 to 2007—reflected the growth of GDP and corporate profit. Profit is enough to spur the stock market, even when wages and salaries are stagnating.

The poor performance of the stock market in 2002 and early 2003 was one of the reasons that corporations were very hesitant about expanding. Seeing your stock going lower and lower does not give confidence. It makes corporations worried about the acceptance of new products and the quantity of products from expanded facilities. When the stock market started to rise on a more or less continuous basis over each full year, this provided some new investment funds. It also provided some of the optimism needed for new corporate investments.

### Stocks in the Great Recession, 2007 to 2009

In the Great Recession that is going on right now in 2009 stocks have fallen more than 50 percent, but they fell 89 percent in the Great Depression. In addition to removing money from consumption and from investment, a fall in the stock market also destroys the confidence of corporate investors, so it makes recovery far more difficult.

The Great Recession began in the fall of 2007. How have stocks behaved in the Great Recession? Their behavior is shown clearly in Figure 8.12.

Figure 8.12 tells a dismal story about the stock market in the Great Recession. Of the five quarters in the graph, two show a very slight expansion of stock prices as profit expanded slightly. Then, however, the economy grew worse. In the fourth quarter of 2008, in which GDP and profit took a nosedive, the stock market crashed and lost value at an annual rate of 70 percent.

In other words, as the economy declined, so did the stock market, but more rapidly. The real economy and the stock market are not the same thing. They do influence each other. The falling stock market reduced the confidence and willingness to buy anything by all those people who owned stocks.

### Appendix 8.3: How Janet Predicted the Stock Market

Janet, a friend of the author, sold all her holdings of stock in August 2007, near the peak of the stock market, and about five months before the Great Recession began in December 2007. (Janet's name is fictitious, but the story is true.) Janet did not guess the correct time to sell her stock by magic or any supernatural means.

To some extent, it is possible to predict, within a wide window of time, the beginning of an economic Great Recession or a very strong recession. By looking for the right clues, and if the gaps and disproportions already there are strong enough, people can tell that some kind of contraction is coming in the near future. Seeing these clues depends on an approach that understands the cycle downturns as the result of internal dynamics within the economic expansion.

Most economists do not look for such clues. The reason is that they believe that the economic institutions of capitalism are self-regulating. In Chapter 1,

Figure 8.12   **Stocks in the Crisis, 2007.4–2008.4**

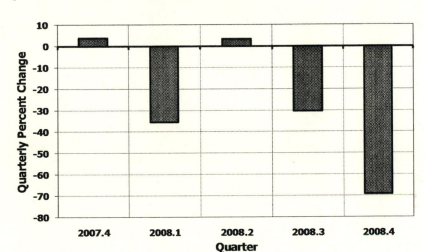

*Source:* Yahoo finance (www.yahoo.com).

*Note:* Stocks means Standard and Poor's 500 corporation stock index, percent change, quarter to quarter, 2007.4 to 2008.4, monthly data aggregated to quarterly data, at annual rates.

Alan Greenspan was quoted as saying that he thought the economy was self-regulating; so neither he nor any other economist predicted such a crisis and contraction. Economists like Greenspan, who believed that there is no internal dynamic leading to a recession, will naturally not look for any clues of this process. This seeming blindness occurs even if the process goes on before their eyes and even if they have expert knowledge of all the facts. Many economists are brilliant, so the problem is only the blindness of ideological dogma.

Janet, on the contrary, has an approach based on the view that recessions result from the internal dynamics of each expansion under capitalist economic institutions. Thus, she was looking very hard for such clues. Here is what she found in 2007.

First, because the same sequence leads from every expansion to recession or depression, it is possible to construct an index of eight or nine economic series that always turn down six to nine months before the cycle peaks. This simple forecasting system, based on the work of the economist Wesley Mitchell, is called the leading indicators. Several such indexes are available. A good one is published weekly by the Economic Cycle Research Institute (ECRI) at www.businesscycle.com. Such an index is a good indicator of the general direction of the economy. Yet it leaves open a wide range of times for a turning point, either peak or trough, to happen. Any weekly change could be just a blip of no consequence. This is not an easy road to riches in the stock market.

Second, in every cycle wages and salaries lag far behind profit income (see Chapter 4). This puts limits on mass purchasing power for consumer goods and services. Thus, it leads to lower profit in the whole sector of consumer goods and services (see Chapter 5).

Third, in every cycle the gross domestic product (see Chapter 3) and aggregate U.S. consumption (see Chapter 5) rise in the early expansion fairly rapidly, but then have a declining growth rate in the last stages of expansion.

Fourth, the prices of raw materials, such as oil, rise very rapidly in the last half of the expansion (see Chapter 10). In this period, raw material prices rise far more rapidly than consumer goods prices, so this is a drag on profit in many sectors.

Fifth, government taxes rise much more rapidly in the last half of the expansion than does government spending, so government gives less and less stimulus to the economy—and may even depress the economy by running a surplus, as it did in 1999 and 2000 (see Chapter 9).

Sixth, in the last part of the expansion, imports usually let money flow out of the U.S. economy faster than exports bring a flow into the economy (see Chapter 10).

Seventh, interest rates usually rise in the last part of the expansion, creating an obstacle to the use of credit for consumer spending and for investment spending (see Chapter 8).

In addition to these seven clues of a recession, Janet found three other clues that the recession might become a Great Recession. She found that housing sales were declining (see Chapter 6), that excessive rivers of credit were weakening the financial system (see Chapter 8), and that all other major industrial countries were also beginning to show these signs in slowing growth (in the leading indicators for other countries).

Janet was clearly very smart to see the signs in the economy and to act on them in the stock market. She was, however, also very lucky because she was studying the business cycle in depth just about six months before the Great Recession began. At such a time, the signs of an imminent collapse are strong and clear. At most other times, prediction of the next major movement to come soon in the economy is best left to fools, while following such predictions by speculating in the stock market is best left to big fools.

# 9

# Government Spending and Taxes

How has the role of government in the economy dramatically changed since World War II? How has government spending and taxation actually behaved over the business cycle?

### Government: The Vested Interests and the Public Interest

The great historical contribution of the United States is that its political process is democratic in form. It has free elections in which no group is excluded and every citizen has one vote. Elections are designed to follow the majority vote, but there are constitutional provisions protecting the rights of the minority to freedom of speech and organization.

The economic system is very different. As demonstrated in Chapter 4, a small wealthy minority—less than 1 percent of the population—owns most of the corporate stock. They appoint the executives, and the executives run the corporations as an absolute dictatorship. There is tremendous inequality of income and wealth. This situation in the economy means that wealthy individuals and corporations have an enormous influence in the political sphere.

The most important vested interest groups are the wealthy individuals and the giant corporations. The best example of vested interests is the interest of the insurance companies in keeping the present health insurance system. They make hundreds of billions of profits and their rate of profit is far above the U.S. average. The public interest has been put forth by President Obama in the form of a public option that would allow the average person to choose a public plan that would be much less expensive than the private plans. The insurance companies are fighting this consumer option tooth and nail.

The health insurance companies are spending hundreds of millions of dollars to convince people of a series of lies about the public plan. For example, they claim it would give money to illegal immigrants. That is simply false. They claim that it would have a "death panel" of government bureaucrats to oversee every senior person to determine how long they will be allowed to live. That is simply false. On the contrary, there is money in the plan to allow an elderly person to get advice on how to control his/her own fate in an emergency.

It is a mistake, however, to think that the banks and other giant corporations can do as they please. Many popular movements have achieved reforms, as was true under President Franklin Roosevelt in the Great Depression and under President Obama in the Great Recession. Such reforms have greatly improved conditions, but they have not changed the nature of the basic political and economic institutions of the United States.

The next few sections will show that the government spends and taxes according to economic conditions along with the struggle between the vested interests and popular movements.

**Changes in the Structure of Government Taxes and Spending**

While the U.S. government has always affected the economy in many ways, an essentially new relationship has emerged since the United States entered World War II in 1941. In 1929 the federal government spent only 1 percent of GDP, but it spent 40 percent of GDP during the war by 1943. The government has become an extremely large source of demand for goods and services, from bombs to toilet seats. The newly emerged economic structure is dominated not only by large private corporations, but also by pervasive governmental spending, mostly centered on three activities: military production, the provision of retirement and health care benefits for the elderly, and saving the private economy from crisis. The U.S. economy is no longer an exclusively private economy.

**The Structural Trend of Government Spending, 1970 to 2001**

How much does government spend? What was the trend in government spending in the period from 1970 to 2001? There were five business cycles in that period. In the first cycle, that of 1970 to 1975, total spending by the federal government and all local and state governments amounted to an average $918 billion per year. In the last cycle, that of 1990 to 2001, total government spending at all levels of government was $1,469 billion per year, a very large increase. These amounts and all dollar amounts of government spending in this chapter are in real terms—that is, the dollars are calculated after adjustment for inflation.

## Discretionary and Automatic Government Spending

Fiscal policy is defined as decisions on government spending and taxing. Those types of spending that are deeply imbedded in the country's present political fundamentals and legal structure, such as Social Security, are called automatic fiscal policy. Congress does not need to vote on Social Security every year. The payments are made every year unless Congress changes the system.

Many items of spending are fixed in concrete in the budget because they are inherited from prior commitments made in the laws by the government. For example, in the 1930s, the Democratic administration of President Roosevelt decided to provide unemployment compensation for those who were unemployed. There would be a firestorm if a new administration tried to eliminate unemployment compensation altogether after all these years. Of course, the government can change the amount of compensation.

As another example, Social Security payments were also pledged in the 1930s. The federal government can change the amount to a small degree. If, however, Congress voted to eliminate Social Security altogether, there would be a political earthquake. Any Congress members who favored such a measure would disappear in the next election. In fact, President George W. Bush tried for some years with all the power of the presidency to push a campaign to change Social Security from fixed payments to recipients to a new program of private investments in the stock market. He called this plan a reform to "save" Social Security. Most people, however, felt that it would have destroyed Social Security as a secure retirement fund. The more he spoke about it, the lower his popularity became. Therefore, even the Republican Congress of that time did not seriously consider it.

Congress has discretion to spend what is left after automatic spending is covered by the budget. Since the automatic spending is much larger than discretionary spending, the course of government spending has the same pattern in almost every peacetime cycle.

The pattern of spending and taxing over the peacetime business cycle changes when there is a large war. Large wars are financed by discretionary spending. This is especially true since nonmilitary, domestic discretionary spending, including social spending such as support for low-income housing, and infrastructure expenditures, such as the electrical grid, has been slashed. In 1978, federal domestic discretionary spending was 4.8 percent of GDP. It was just 3.4 percent of GDP in 2008. The following sections will describe what government has actually done in spending in the average business cycle.

## Definition and Impact of Deficit Spending

Federal deficit spending happens whenever federal spending is greater than federal taxes. Most federal revenue comes from taxes, so for simplicity the word "taxes" is used in this chapter to mean all revenue.

In the short run, deficit spending certainly stimulates the economy because it means more money flowing into the economy from government than is taken out in taxes. However, there are problems. First, the deficit must not be too small to stimulate the economy nor too large to overheat it. Second, some payments, such as teachers' salaries, provide more stimulus than other payments, such as money that will go into the vaults of a bank and just sit there. Third, the long-run effect of an increase in the national debt is that more money goes from the average taxpayer to the wealthy person who owns the debt, so there is more inequality.

## Government Spending in Five Cycles, 1970 to 2001

In the average expansion of the previous five cycles, from 1970 to 2001, the amount of government spending rose in every stage of expansion, but it rose more slowly than GDP. This section considers why government spending rose in expansions. Then it considers why government spending rose more slowly than GDP. All data here are real—that is, adjusted for inflation. The data on government cyclical behavior are portrayed in Figure 9.1.

What does Figure 9.1 say about federal spending? During the average expansion, federal spending rose slowly over the whole expansion. The continuous but slow rise of government spending in expansions was not mysterious because there is always a need for expanding or improving some government function. For example, there is always a need for new or improved roads and bridges.

Government revenue rose as incomes increased in the expansions in this period, so it was easy to spend some portion on important projects. The expansion of government revenue and spending continued regardless of which party was in power and regardless of what was promised by candidates.

Figure 9.1 also shows that government spending continued to climb in economic contractions. Most sectors of the economy fall in recessions, so why does government spending rise? The answer is that automatic spending has been built-in by laws over many decades. For example, the government gives compensation to unemployed workers if they were fired through no fault of their own. Unemployment increases as firms fire workers because there is no demand for their products. Therefore, government compensation to unemployed workers automatically increases in recessions.

Figure 9.1 **Federal Spending by Cycle, 1970–2001**

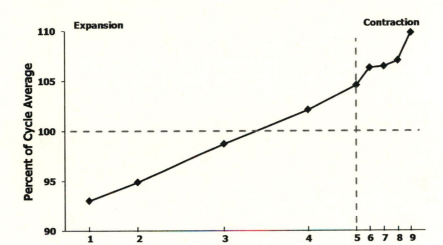

*Source:* Department of Commerce, Bureau of Economic Analysis, NIPA table 3.2, line 39, and NIPA table 1.1.9, line 21 (www.bea.gov).

*Note:* Federal spending is all U.S. government expenditures on goods and services. Average of five cycles, 1970.4 to 2001.4, billions of dollars, adjusted for inflation by the federal implicit price deflator of the Department of Commerce. Seasonally adjusted quarterly data at annual rates.

Some welfare spending is given by law to those who are too poor to buy necessities such as food. The best example is the issuing of food stamps to the poor. Therefore, welfare spending automatically increases in recessions because the number of poor people always increases in recessions.

For these reasons, automatic government spending rose during the previous five recessions. What is even more remarkable is that the automatic increases in government spending not only cause an increase in the amount, but also in the growth rate of spending in recessions. In the five cycles from 1970 to 2001, during the average economic expansion, federal government spending rose rather slowly at 1.8 percent per year. This rate of growth was far slower than the rise of GDP in those expansions. During the same period, in the average recession, however, government spending rose much faster at 6 percent a year. Thus, federal government spending rises only slowly in expansions but rapidly in contractions.

One conclusion is that the business cycle automatically changes the pattern of government spending from relatively slow in expansions to relatively fast

117

in contractions. This is so in every cycle except when there are enormous changes in discretionary spending, such as during wars. During a major war, discretionary spending for military commodities swamps the change in automatic spending, so the result is very different than in peacetime recessions.

The second conclusion is that government spending will have a different effect on aggregate demand in expansions than in contractions. Remember, government spending is a part of total or aggregate demand. When government spending rises more slowly than GDP in peacetime expansions, it contributes only a little to the growth of aggregate demand.

In fact, since government spending falls further as a percentage of GDP in the late stages of expansion, it has less effect on holding demand up to the level of the total GDP supplied to the market. As private spending weakens and rises more slowly near the peak of the cycle, the slower government spending growth also weakens the growth of demand.

In recessions, however, when government spending rises rapidly, it is one of the things that help stimulate the economy and start a new recovery. On the other hand, there were many economic recoveries in American history before government played a significant role. Therefore, government spending was not the sole cause of recovery in many recessions. However, the increased government spending did help the private sector to recover a little faster than it might otherwise have done.

Whether government spending is good or bad for the economy is discussed in Chapter 12.

## Government Taxation in the Five Cycles, 1970 to 2001

Government spending is only half the picture. The other half is taxes. Taxation behaves quite differently from government spending and is much easier to understand. Federal taxes rise when people have more income. Federal income taxes are some fixed percentage at every level of income. They are called "progressive" because the percentage of taxation increases as the income bracket increases.

Under President Roosevelt's Democratic administration in World War II, the tax percentage rose steeply as income rose and the income tax was expanded into a broad-based tax to help finance the war. The tax was then very progressive. After the war, under several conservative Republican presidents, the tax rates on the rich were sharply reduced. Therefore, the federal income tax has become much less progressive.

It should also be noted that the federal income tax is a great deal less progressive in reality than it looks on paper. The problem is that there are major loopholes for high-income earners. For example, if a rich person owns

Figure 9.2   **Federal Revenue (Mostly Taxes) by Cycle, 1970–2001**

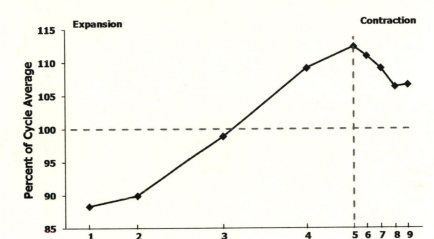

*Source:* Department of Commerce, Bureau of Economic Analysis, NIPA table 3.2, line 36, and NIPA table 1.1.9, line 21 (www.bea.gov).

*Note:* Federal revenue consists of all payments to the government in the form of taxes and fees. Average of five cycles, 1970.4 to 2001.4, billions of current dollars, adjusted by the federal implicit price deflator. Seasonally adjusted quarterly data, at annual rates.

stock in a corporation, and sells it after a few years at a big profit, it is called a capital gain. Capital gains from stocks are charged a lower tax rate than the ordinary income tax rate.

Although President George W. Bush made the federal tax less progressive, the federal income tax is still progressive. It is progressive enough that when national income rises and most people go into higher tax brackets, the government not only collects higher taxes, but also actually collects a higher percentage of income. On the other hand, when there is a recession, most taxpayers have lower income, so they pay a lower percentage of their income in taxes.

The cyclical behavior of the federal income tax is shown in Figure 9.2. Because it is progressive, the federal income tax tends to rise rapidly in expansions, but to fall rapidly in recessions. Figure 9.2 shows that taxes rose when national income rose in an expansion. On the other hand, federal income taxes fell when income fell in a recession.

In fact, income taxes rise somewhat faster than national income in an expansion. Income taxes, however, also fall somewhat faster than national income in a recession.

Table 9.1

**Federal Taxes, Spending, and Deficit, 1970–2001**
(percent change in expansion and contraction)

| | Expansion Stage 5 minus Stage 1 | Contraction Stage 9 minus Stage 5 |
|---|---|---|
| Spending | 11.5 | 5.2 |
| Taxes | 24.0 | −5.8 |
| Deficit | −12.5 | 11.0 |

*Source:* Bureau of Economic Analysis, Department of Commerce (www.bea.gov).

*Note:* Spending is real federal government total expenditures. Taxes are real federal government total receipts. Both are adjusted by the federal price deflator. Both are average of five cycles, 1970 to 2001, in billions of chained 2000 dollars, seasonally adjusted. Expansion is percent change from initial trough to cycle peak. Contraction is percent change from cycle peak to final trough. Deficit is spending minus taxes.

Higher taxes on the average person mean less demand for goods and services. Lower taxes on the average person mean more demand for goods and services. The issue in Congress is always which class gets lower or higher taxes, the employee class or the wealthy owners of corporations. There have been many titanic battles in Congress over this issue.

It matters which class gets a tax cut. Under President Bush, most tax cuts went to the rich and few or no tax cuts to the employee class. But the rich spend less of their income than the employee class on consumer goods. It follows that if the rich are given a big tax cut, it does little or nothing to increase consumer spending.

**The Federal Deficit, 1970 to 2001**

Federal spending and taxes have been examined and have shown a clear cyclical pattern, repeated in each peacetime cycle. The effect of this pattern on the federal deficit is revealed in Table 9.1. The table shows that in the expansion in the average of the previous five cycles, from 1970 through 2001, spending rose less than half as much as taxes. Spending means that dollars flow out of the federal government, so they tend to make for a higher deficit. But taxes are a flow of money from people to the government, so they tend to lower the deficit.

Since taxes are rising faster than federal spending in the average expansion, the deficit must fall in the average expansion. Indeed, the Table 9.1 shows that the deficit did fall very considerably in the average expansion. Federal spending was able to rise, even with a falling deficit, because taxes rose so fast.

Figure 9.3  **Federal Spending by Year, 2001–2008**

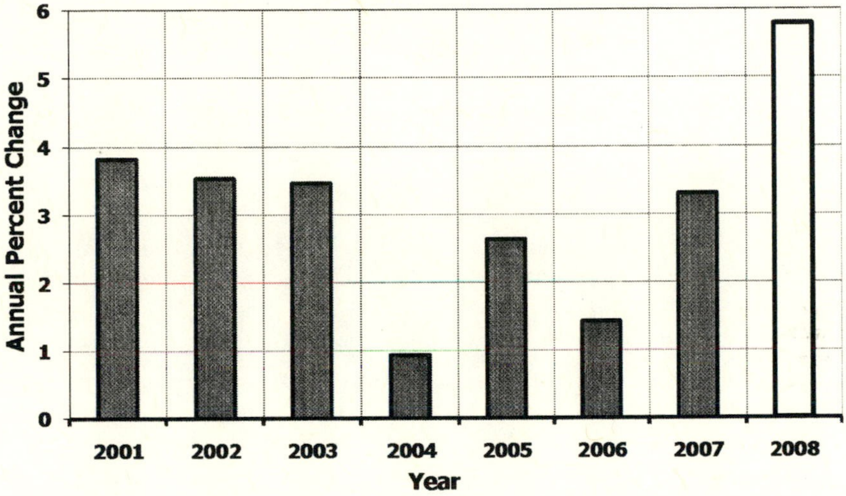

*Source:* Department of Commerce, Bureau of Economic Analysis, NIPA table 3.2, line 39, and NIPA table 1.1.9, line 21 (www.bea.gov).

*Note:* Federal spending is all U.S. government expenditures on goods and services. Percent change, year-to-year, 2001 to 2008, in billions of current dollars, adjusted by the federal implicit price deflator.

Matters were quite different in the average recession of these five cycles. Federal spending rose rapidly, while taxes fell considerably. Since the flow of money into government from people was falling, while the flow of money to the people was rapidly rising, the deficit has to rise rapidly. According to arithmetic, it is a sad fact that when spending rises and taxes fall, the deficit must rise.

In other words, in the average recession government has a smaller flow of money coming in, but a bigger flow of money going out. Therefore, the table shows a rising deficit in the average recession. The rise of government deficit spending, as pointed out earlier, will stimulate the economy. The most important problem with the rising deficit is that it means greater inequality since the bondholders are wealthy individuals, while the payer is the average taxpayer.

**Government Spending in the Bush Expansion and the Great Recession**

Figure 9.3 shows that government spending in the Bush administration followed the same general rules. This figure reveals that in the middle of the

121

expansion, when GDP was rising most rapidly, government spending rose only about 1 percent a year. Spending growth simply rose relatively slowly to cope with growing population and other normal problems.

On the other hand, federal spending rose far more rapidly in the recession year of 2001 and the Great Recession years of 2008 and 2009. Why does government spending rise rapidly in recessions? As explained in the earlier section on spending in previous recessions, the federal government automatically spends more in any contraction. The increases stem from various automatic spending laws, such as unemployment compensation.

In addition to the normal reasons for higher federal spending, there was also some increase in 2003 to 2008 for war spending. Finally, President Bush in 2008 began the process of giving away hundreds of billions of dollars to the banks and other financial organizations. Some of that money showed up as government spending, but much of it was outside the budget through the Federal Reserve. There was only a small stimulus package for the economy under President Bush, so that does not appear as a major effect in 2008.

## Taxes in the Expansion and Great Recession, 2001 to 2009

In the previous five cycles, taxes moved with income, so they rose in expansions and fell in contractions. This point is also illustrated in Figure 9.4 showing the data on taxes (including fees and other revenues) for the expansion of 2001 to 2007, plus the first full year of the crisis in 2008. This figure emphasizes that taxes behave just the opposite of spending in most cycles, except for cycles of unlimited warfare. Beginning in the recession of 2001, tax revenues went down for three years. Tax revenues went down for those three years because national income and GDP were very weak for those three years, as shown in earlier chapters. Also the Bush administration passed a massive pro-rich tax cut in 2001. Furthermore, most income tax payments come a year after the income was received. That is why the impact of the recession shows most strongly in 2002, not 2001.

Figure 9.4 also shows quite clearly that tax payments to the government declined in 2008, as a result of the crisis. Of course, these payments reflect 2007 income when the contraction was just beginning; so it is not a large decline. The large decline will come in the 2009 taxes, reflecting the crisis of 2008. The dramatic drop in tax revenues will push the federal budget further into the red and open up massive deficits in state and local government budgets as well.

Figure 9.4 **Federal Revenue (Mostly Taxes) by Year, 2001–2008**

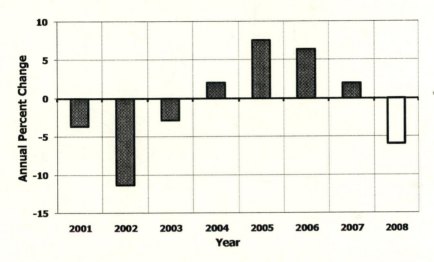

*Source:* Department of Commerce, Bureau of Economic Analysis, NIPA table 3.2, line 36, and NIPA table 1.1.9, line 21 (www.bea.gov).

*Note:* Federal revenue consists of all payments to the government in the form of taxes and fees. Percent change, year-to-year, 2001 to 2008, in billions of current dollars, adjusted by the federal implicit price deflator.

### The Deficit in the Expansion and Great Recession, 2001 to 2009

In the expansion under President Clinton in the 1990s, the deficit became a surplus in his second term. Then in the recession of 2001, there was again a significant deficit. This fits with the expected cyclical pattern. A part of it, however, was also the product of tight Clinton budgets and the huge Bush tax giveaways to the rich.

Then, in the expansion of 2001–2007, the deficit continued to rise until 2005. This rising deficit in a recovery was unusual. The increase reflected the combination of the Bush tax cuts and the beginning of the spending for the Iraq war. Only in 2005 did the deficit start to fall as in most expansions. In current dollars at the peak of the cycle in the second quarter of 2007, the deficit was running at the rate of $365 billion a year. In the financial crisis, the deficit became much, much worse.

These tendencies can be seen in Figure 9.5. The figure shows that there was no deficit in the first quarter of 2001, when President Bush took office. After that, however, a recession began immediately. Thus federal spending rose rapidly for a couple of years, then more slowly for the rest of the expansion.

Figure 9.5   **Deficit Gap, 2001–2008**

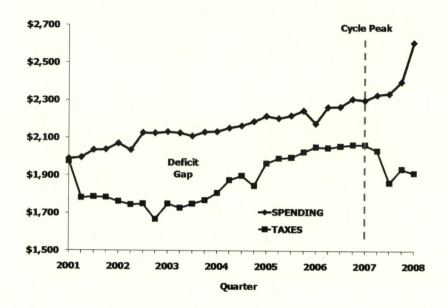

*Source:* Department of Commerce, Bureau of Economic analysis, NIPA table 3.2, lines 36 and 39, and NIPA table 1.1.9, line 21 (www.bea.gov).

*Note:* Spending is all U.S. government expenditures on goods and services. Taxes consist of all payments to the government in the form of taxes and fees. Both series are 2001.4 to 2008.4, in billions of current dollars adjusted by the federal implicit price deflator, quarterly data.

On the contrary, in the recession, since there was less income, tax revenues declined. At the same time, spending increased on such items as unemployment compensation. During the recession and then again after the recession, as noted above, President Bush cut the taxes of the wealthy. Also after the recession, the Bush administration started to spend on the Iraq war. Since taxes were falling, while federal spending was rising, the deficit gap had to get larger. The figure shows the widening gap in those early years.

As the expansion continued more strongly, there was less automatic spending. Thus, the growth rate of federal spending sank to a lower level. Taxes rose fairly rapidly in the middle of the expansion. So the deficit began to fall. The deficit fell or remained constant for the rest of the expansion.

Moreover, the figure reveals the dramatic events of the crisis, from the fourth quarter of 2007 through the fourth quarter of 2008. The economic crisis naturally caused the revenue from income tax payments to fall very considerably.

Table 9.2

**Federal Taxes, Spending, and Deficit, 2001–2008**

|                    | 2001    | 2007    | 2008    |
|--------------------|---------|---------|---------|
| Taxes              | $2,044  | $2,678  | $2,601  |
| Spending           | $2,002  | $2,973  | $3,247  |
| Surplus or deficit | $42     | –$295   | –$646   |

*Source:* Bureau of Economic Analysis, Department of Commerce (www.bea.gov).

*Note:* Spending is federal government total expenditures. Taxes are federal government total receipts. Both are in billions of current dollars, annual data, no deflator. Surplus is taxes minus spending. Deficit is spending minus taxes, and is a negative number.

On the other side, the crisis caused automatic federal spending to rise. Because there was also intentional spending on stimulus to the economy by Congress, federal spending rose very fast. Thus there was a startling rise in the federal deficit in 2008. This was President Bush's legacy to President Obama.

Finally, these trends shown in Figure 9.5 are made clearer with the data in Table 9.2. This simple table presents the data in billions of current dollars. The table shows that for all of 2001, federal spending was a little over $2 trillion. The taxes were larger. So the Clinton budget surpluses continued into this year.

By 2008, in his last year, President Bush spent over $3 trillion, bailing out investments banks, giant insurers, and much of the financial industry. The taxes were much less than that. Therefore the deficit grew to $646 billion for the year.

## What Are the Effects of the Federal Deficit?

Are federal deficits good or bad for the economy? It depends. If the economy is in a recession or depression, the immediate effect of deficit spending is to stimulate the economy and expand jobs.

Suppose there is a deficit of ten dollars because spending is ten dollars more than tax revenue. Suppose the whole ten dollars goes to a woman named Nancy. Suppose that Nancy spends the whole ten dollars on lollipops. This money will go to the owners and workers who make and sell lollipops. Assume they spend 90 percent of it for more consumer goods and services. Their spending will certainly further increase demand for consumer goods and services. So the ten dollars helps stimulate the economy.

But what if the spending is all for war supplies? The war spending stimulates like lollipops, but the long-run result is slower growth discussed in the next section.

What if there is deficit spending during a peacetime expansion? If the economy is not running at full capacity and full employment, then deficit spending can help keep the expansion rolling along, helping to create jobs and business expansion. But the normal course of events is that, as taxes rise in an expansion, deficit spending falls. As it falls, it removes one important support for the economy. So a declining amount of deficit spending is one cause of a weakening economy, which may lead to recession or depression.

In the long run, deficits every year lead to a rising debt. The national debt is held by foreigners and very rich Americans. The higher the debt, the more money that flows from the average taxpayer to wealthy Americans and to wealthy foreigners. The increasing inequality reduces the total buying power of the whole country.

When the national debt is all held by Americans, growing inequality is the main worry. If foreigners own the debt, the problem is much worse. For example, the Chinese own over a trillion dollars of the U.S. national debt. If China decides that the euro is stronger than the dollar, it may start shifting some of that money to Europe. The lack of confidence in the American dollar would make it harder and harder to sell the American debt to anyone.

**The Government Deficit in War and Peace**

In peacetime, the deficit tends to fall in expansions and rise in recessions, as shown above. However, the deficit tends to do the exact opposite in wartime cycles. Why is that?

In wartime, government spending rises rapidly. Government demand for military products (such as bombs) and services (such as soldiers) is virtually unlimited during a large-scale war. For example, in 1938 at the end of the Great Depression, 18 percent of the workforce still lived in miserable unemployment. Yet by 1943 during World War II, there was zero unemployment, except for people moving from one job to another. Frictional unemployment, movement from one job to another in 1943, was only 1 percent of the labor force.

Why was there full employment? It was because the U.S. government spent 40 percent of the GDP on military production and soldiers. That flood of spending used up all the millions of unemployed people and then hunted for more. Indeed, a great many women left their homes during the day to do paid production work for the first time.

The government in World War II, as in all wars, found that it could not raise taxes enough to pay for the war. That always happens because governments do not want to be unpopular in a war, so they are afraid to raise the necessary taxes. In this case, taxes would have had to rise from 1 or 2 percent of the GDP to 40 percent of GDP.

Since government spending zoomed upward, while taxes rose very slowly, there was a huge deficit during World War II. This also happens in every war. At present, the Iraq war has driven military spending to about half a trillion dollars a year. For political reasons, taxes had fallen. Therefore, the war has also produced a record deficit.

Moreover, the operations of the economy pay no attention to the ideology and promises of presidents and political parties. In the expansion of World War II under President Roosevelt, the deficit rose dramatically. In the Korean War, under President Truman, the deficit rose. In the Vietnam War, under President Johnson, the deficit rose. In the two Iraq wars, the first under President George H.W. Bush and the second under his son, President George W. Bush, the deficit rose to what were then record heights.

Yet in all the time since World War II, the deficit has fallen in every peacetime expansion under every president, whether Democrat or Republican. The reason, as shown earlier, is that most government spending is automatic under existing laws. As a result of those laws, government spending rises only very slowly in expansions. However, taxes rise rapidly in every expansion under existing laws. Therefore, in peacetime expansions, the deficit must fall. Only extreme changes in the laws would change this cause and effect. Only in a war does the discretionary spending skyrocket, producing a deficit in an expansion.

Immediately following a war, military spending usually declines rapidly. Thus, in the recession following a war, the deficit will actually decline. Remember that in peacetime recessions, the deficit usually rises.

In the Bush years, military spending for war increased again after declining during the Clinton years in the 1990s. That change is evident in the pattern of federal government purchases.

The federal government spends in two ways. First, the government transfers tax revenues to households, which in turn spend that money. For example, Social Security and Medicare transfer income to the retired. Welfare and Medicaid transfer income to the poor. Interest payments on government bonds transfer money to the wealthy bondholders. Unemployment insurance transfers income to the unemployed.

The government both purchases goods and services from the private sector (e.g., purchasing military armaments) and directly provides services and goods (e.g., building a road). Government spending directly increases economic production, in either the private sector or the public sector.

The division of government purchases between peaceful, non-military spending and military spending has changed dramatically over the years, especially in the last decade. That dramatic difference can be seen in Figure 9.6.

Figure 9.6 **War Gap, 1970–2008**

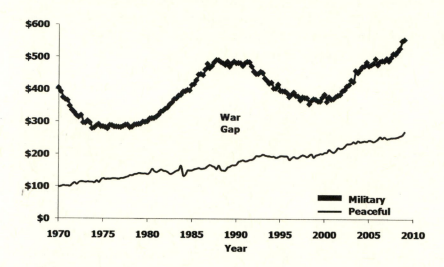

*Source:* Department of Commerce, Bureau of Economic analysis, NIPA table 1.1.5, lines 22 and 23, and NIPA table 1.1.9, lines 22 and 23 (www.bea.gov).

*Note:* War means federal national defense spending and peace means federal non-defense spending. Both series are 1970.4 to 2008.4, in billions of chained 2000 dollars, quarterly data.

The war gap in government purchases is apparent in Figure 9.6. It shows that military purchases exceeded nonmilitary purchases by the federal government during the whole period from 1970 to 2008. The war gap became much larger during the administration of President George H.W. Bush. These government purchases went to the first Iraq war. Then war purchases declined in the Clinton expansion of 1991 to 2000. Figure 9.6 also reveals the rapid rise of military purchases in the Bush expansion of 2001 to 2007.

The importance of military purchases is apparent in the startling contrast between military and nonmilitary, peacetime purchases. In the fourth quarter of 2001 at the beginning of the recovery, peacetime purchases were $225 billion, but military purchases were already $406 billion. Thus, at the beginning of the expansion, there was already a gap between military and nonmilitary purchases. The gap increased over the expansion of 2001 to 2007. While nonmilitary federal purchases rose to $315 billion, war purchases rose far faster to $655 billion by the second quarter of 2007. In that quarter, if military spending for war had been cut in half, the federal deficit would have disappeared.

## The Obama Stimulus and Budget

The first Obama deficit spending came in the stimulus package passed a month after he came to power. Then the first Obama budget, passed in late 2009, covered the next fiscal year and was similar in content to the stimulus package in its projects and large deficit spending for stimulus.

A do-nothing strategy would saddle the federal budget with even larger deficits as the economy and federal tax revenues continue to fall. Although the stimulus to the economy from deficit spending under President Obama helped the economy to recover, it was not sufficient to stop unemployment from rising for many more months.

## Inside the Obama Budget

The effects of taxation and spending depend, not just on the totals, but also on who gets taxed and where the money is spent. The first Obama budget passed by Congress reduced taxes for most people in the country, as Obama had promised in his election campaign. Those middle-class tax cuts included a child tax credit and education incentives for income tax payers. The Obama administration's payroll tax holiday will benefit the bottom 60 percent of taxpayers. From the viewpoint of consumer spending, those tax cuts are very good because the average American will spend more money per dollar of income for consumption than the rich will spend on consumption per dollar of income.

On the spending side, the Obama budget provides much needed spending on infrastructure (such as roads and bridges), education, health care, and energy. This kind of spending will normally produce more stimuli per dollar of spending than tax cuts. The money spent on roads is soon re-spent by the workers and contractors who receive it, so that multiplies its effect.

Government spending on green energy projects, which will increase energy while preventing pollution, will benefit the economy in the long run. In the short run, it will help stimulate jobs and production. Similarly, government spending on roads and bridges helps short-run job growth, but it will also provide a healthier economic growth in the future.

Nonetheless, infrastructure spending in the Obama budget falls well short of what is needed. The American Society of Civil Engineers assigned an overall grade of D to the nation's infrastructure. Engineers estimate that it would take a $2.2 trillion investment over the next five years to bring the infrastructure into a state of good repair. All discretionary domestic spending in the FY2010 budget, of which infrastructure spending is just one of many parts, is less than one quarter of that amount.

Education spending has two important functions. Schools need construction workers to build them and teachers to work in them, so it stimulates the economy. Furthermore, education helps individuals to develop to their fullest potential, which helps society to have a faster growing economy. Education expenditures have a track record of being an effective way to stimulate a slumping economy.

Health care has the same attributes as education. Hospitals require construction workers initially, but they also require doctors and nurses. Better health care allows people to live longer and better lives. Better health also allows the economy to grow faster because employees are off work less for sickness. The Obama administration has passed a major bill to have universal health care, discussed in the next chapter.

**Clues to Remember**

Before the Great Depression and World War II, government spending and taxes were a tiny part of GDP. Since that time, government spending and taxes have been a large percentage of GDP, so it has played a major role in the economy.

This chapter demonstrated that in every peacetime expansion period, taxes rose faster than spending. Therefore, deficit spending slowly declined toward the end of every expansion. The decline of government deficit spending reduced the flow of money to the economy and hastened the recession. In the last half of the Bush expansion, the same pattern emerged. Taxes rose, the deficit fell, and the growth of aggregate demand was reduced.

In every peacetime recession, taxes fell faster than spending. Therefore, deficit spending rose, which helped to stimulate the economy.

As in all previous recessions, the deficit during the recession was increased under President Bush and then increased further under President Obama. What is different is the incredible magnitude of the deficit in the Great Recession of 2007 to 2009. The reader will have to wait until the policy chapter, Chapter 12, for an evaluation of whether this was good policy or not.

# 10

# The Trade Gap

## How Boom and Bust Spread Around the Globe

Previous chapters have discussed three spending flows that purchase the GDP. They are the flows from consumers, investors, and government. This chapter examines the fourth and last spending flow to buy GDP. The fourth flow is called net exports, which is exports minus imports.

**What Are Exports and Imports?**

U.S. exports are those goods and services that Americans sell abroad. Someone in Germany who wants a Dell computer can buy it at a local store. How did the computer get to the store? When the supply of Dell computers in Germany gets too low, the storekeeper asks Dell to send more computers. Dell then exports computers to Germany. In exchange for the computers, the German store sends money to Dell.

The German store has imported computers. Imports are goods and services purchased from abroad. In order to import, it is necessary to send money abroad.

When an American corporation receives money from abroad, it uses the money to pay employees, give dividends to stockholders, and buy investment goods to expand its business. Exports lead to a flow of money into America. The increased income to Americans results in an increase in demand for American goods and services. Some of the increased demand for U.S. commodities comes directly from the foreigners who buy the exported goods and services. There will be additional demand from the corporation's owners and employees that receive the money from abroad.

Similarly, when an American company imports goods and services from abroad, it pays out money to foreign businesses. Therefore, imports diminish the demand for American commodities. If an American buys a Volkswagen car from Germany, the car comes to the United States. The money flows to Germany as demand for German automobiles. In other words, exports bring a flow of money into the United States, but imports send a flow of money out of the United States.

Net exports are the dollar value of exports minus the dollar value of imports. When exports are larger than imports, net exports are positive. A positive amount of net exports is called a trade surplus. A U.S. trade surplus means that goods are flowing out of America and money is flowing into America.

If imports are greater than exports, then net exports are negative. In that case, money is flowing out of America and there is a trade deficit. By pulling money out of the United States, the trade deficit reduces the demand for goods and services in the American market.

### Trends in the Structure of U.S. Trade

For about 100 years, from roughly 1870 to 1970, the United States exported more than it imported. Thus, net exports were positive in that whole period. This was a trade surplus. Every year, American goods and services flowed to foreign countries, while money flowed into America. In other words, the trade surplus (or positive net exports) increased demand in America by that net inflow of money.

Since about 1970, however, imports have been greater than exports. There is a trade deficit pulling money out of America every year. This is illustrated in Figure 10.1.

The trade deficit has grown larger over time. In the first cycle of this period, 1970 to 1975, the trade deficit was $61 billion. This meant a trade gap to be filled by the flow of $61 billion in American money out of the country. This weakens demand for American goods and services.

In the most recent cycle of this period, from 1991 to 2001, the trade deficit was $169 billion. This trade gap meant that all of these billions were rushing out of the country and lowering demand in the United States.

In 2001, the first year of President George W. Bush's administration, the trade gap was $367 billion. By the last year of the Bush administration, in 2008, the trade deficit was $671 billion. That is why Figure 10.1 shows an enormous trade gap. The gap had grown to a very significant part of GDP and had a very negative effect on demand for the internal U.S. market for goods and services.

Figure 10.1 **Trade Gap, 1970–2008**

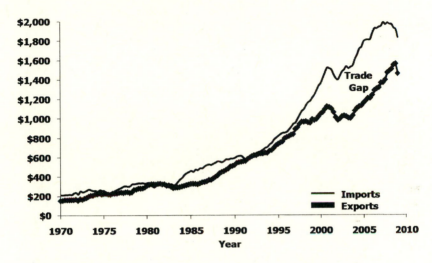

*Source:* Bureau of Economic Analysis, U.S. Department of Commerce (www.bea.gov).

*Note:* Imports are all goods and services imported into the United States. Exports are all goods and services of the United States sold to foreigners. Both series are in billions of chained 2000 dollars, seasonally adjusted, quarterly data.

## Cyclical Behavior of Imports

The long-run trend was clear in the previous section. Now the question is this: how do exports and imports behave over the business cycle? Figure 10.2 shows the behavior of imports over the previous five cycles from 1970 to 2001. The graph shows that imports rose rapidly throughout the average expansion. Imports then fell somewhat in the average contraction. In fact, imports rise and fall with the cycle every time.

Imports are easy to understand and very predictable. Whenever the national income of the United States rises, Americans spend more money on imports. When there is a recession, Americans have less money and they spend less on imports.

## Exports, 1970 to 2001

American exports to the rest of the world do not depend on U.S. demand, but on world demand for U.S. goods and services. When a company in Singapore buys an American computer, U.S. exports rise. Export demand cannot be

Figure 10.2 **Imports by Cycle, 1970–2001**

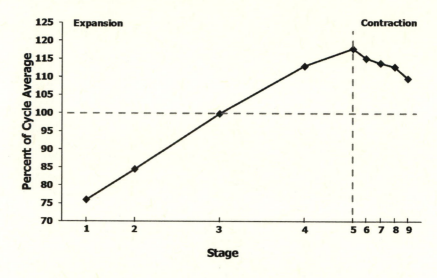

*Source:* U.S. Department of Commerce, Bureau of Economic analysis (www.bea.gov).

*Note:* Imports are all goods and services imported into the United States. Average of five cycles, 1970.4 to 2001.4, billions of chained 2000 dollars, seasonally adjusted, quarterly data.

easily predicted. Usually, American cycles coincide with those of the rest of the world, as shown below. Therefore, exports usually rise somewhat during American expansions and fall somewhat during American recessions. The up and down movements of exports are sluggish because many other things are happening in the rest of the world, so the correlation with American cycles is far from perfect.

The actual movement of exports in the average cycle from 1970 to 2001 is shown in Figure 10.3. Figure 10.3 shows that in the average business cycle expansion during the previous five cycles, the value of exports rose steadily. This meant a growing demand for American products in every expansion. This usual rise of American exports in the expansion is a help to American business. Rising exports, however, is not the only thing happening.

The figure also shows that in the average contraction, American exports decline a little. This means less money coming into American firms, so American wages, salaries, and profits are hurt. This decline in income is harmful to domestic demand for American goods and services.

Figure 10.3 **Exports by Cycle, 1970–2001**

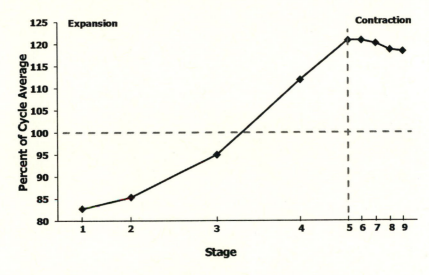

*Source:* U.S. Department of Commerce, Bureau of Economic Analysis
(www.bea.gov).
*Note:* Exports are all goods and services of the United States sold to foreigners. Average of five cycles, 1970.4 to 2001.4, billions of chained 2000 dollars, seasonally adjusted, quarterly data.

## Trade Deficit

Net exports have been negative since 1970. America has a growing trade deficit. This trade gap has resulted in outflows of money and less purchasing power at home. What has been the behavior of the trade deficit over the business cycle?

As shown above, imports and exports both rise in the expansion, while they both decline in the contraction of the average cycle from 1970 to 2001. The question is whether they rise and decline at the same speed, leaving the deficit constant. They actually rise and fall differently on the average.

Imports rose about 40 percent in the average expansion. Exports rose only about 36 percent (see data in Figure 10.2). In the average recession, imports fell about 7 percent, but exports fell only about 5 percent.

The differences are not great in the percentages. They do persist, however, cycle after cycle. First, it is astonishing that the two rise and fall together so closely. This means that the economies of the rest of the world are closely entangled with the American economy. This is so because imports represent

Figure 10.4 **Imports by Year, 2001–2008**

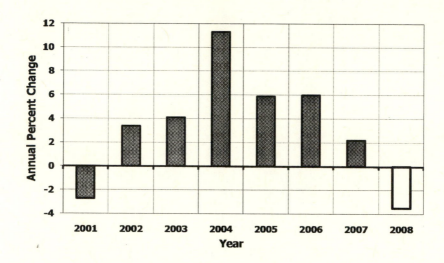

*Source:* U.S. Department of Commerce, Bureau of Economic Analysis (www.bea.gov).

*Note:* Imports are all goods and services imported into the United States. Percent change, year-to-year, 2001 to 2008, in billions of chained 2000 dollars.

American demand, while exports represent demand from the rest of the world. In most cycles, the American economy, being the largest, has tended to lead the others both up and down.

On the other hand, these data show that imports tend to rise and fall faster than exports. The obvious reason is that U.S. imports follow the American cycles exactly. The rest of the world, on the other hand, does not always follow the American lead exactly, whether in the amplitude of the cycle or in the timing of the cycle. Therefore, exports to foreign countries usually do not rise or fall as fast as American imports.

What was the impact of the trade deficit on the end of expansions and the beginning of recessions? First, since about 1970, there has been a trade deficit, tending to increase over time. This is a drag on the U.S. economy because it sends a flow of money overseas that could be used to prop up demand at home. Second, toward the end of each expansion, there was an increase in the trade deficit beyond the long-run trend. That meant a great flow of money away from this country at a time when it could be least afforded. It helped reduce the demand for American goods and services and helped create a big hole just before the recession.

Figure 10.5 **Exports by Year, 2001–2008**

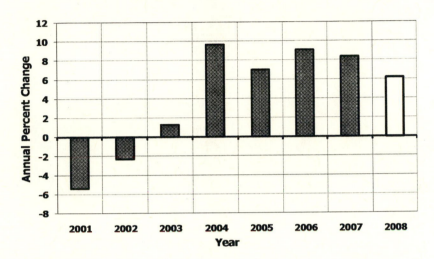

*Source:* U.S. Department of Commerce, Bureau of Economic Analysis (www.bea.gov).
*Note:* Exports are all goods and services of the United States sold to foreigners. Percent change, year-to-year, 2001 to 2008, in billions of chained 2000 dollars.

## Exports and Imports in the Expansion and Great Recession, 2007 to 2009

What happened to exports and imports in the cycle under President Bush, including the expansion of 2001 to 2007 and the Great Recession of 2007 to 2009? The answer as to imports is shown with great clarity in Figure 10.4. The pattern of U.S. imports is so clear that it looks as if mythological numbers were used to make a point. However, this graph uses the actual numbers from the Department of Commerce to find the percentage change year to year.

The figure shows that U.S. imports fell both in the recession of 2001 and in the crisis of 2008. Imports fell because national income fell.

In the expansion, the rate of growth of imports rose for three years and then fell for three years. This was exactly what happened to such aggregate variables as GDP, national income, consumption, and investment.

Imports proceeded in a very clear and systematic way to respond to national income. What happened to exports? Exports are shown in Figure 10.5.

U.S. exports, which represented all foreign demand, acted differently from

Figure 10.6 **Exports and Imports in the Crisis, 2007.4–2008.4**

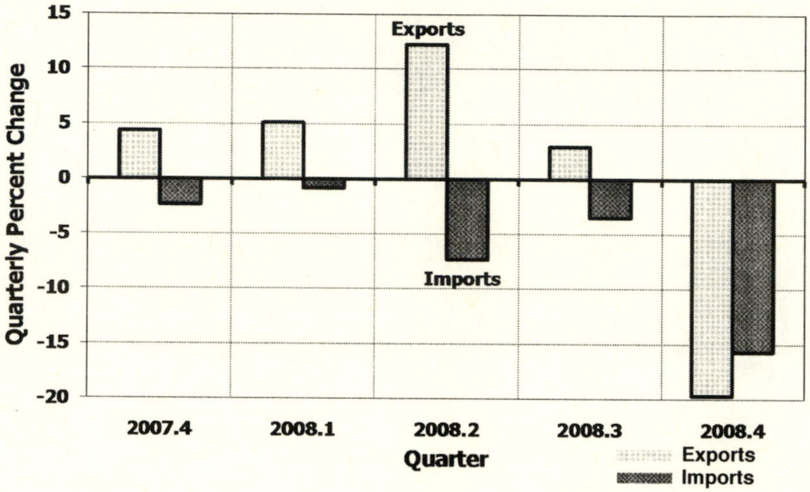

*Source:* U.S. Department of Commerce, Bureau of Economic Analysis
(www.bea.gov).

*Note:* Imports are all goods and services imported into the United States. Exports are
all goods and services of the United States sold to foreigners. Percent change, quarter to
quarter, 2007.4 to 2008.4, in billions of chained 2000 dollars, seasonally adjusted quarterly
data, at annual rates.

U.S. imports, which reflected U.S. demand. Exports fell in 2001 and 2002,
and then were almost constant for the rest of the expansion.

Exports and imports diverged by the end of the expansion in 2007, imports were still rising faster than exports. Since exports bring money in,
while imports send money out of the United States, this meant that more and
more money flowed out of the country. This deficit, or trade gap, meant less
money available for internal U.S. demand for goods and services. The large
and increasing trade gap was, therefore, one reason for the Great Recession
of 2007 to 2009.

The deep decline of American trade in the Great Recession to date is presented dramatically in Figure 10.6. For the first four quarters of the U.S. Great
Recession of 2007 to 2009, American imports were falling. The reason was
that American national income was falling, so the imports also had to fall.

At the same time, in the first year of the Great Recession exports still
continued to rise, moving in the opposite direction from imports. What this

Table 10.1

**Imports, Exports, and Trade Gap, 2001–2008**

|  | 2001 | 2007 | 2008 |
|---|---|---|---|
| Exports | $1,033 | $1,662 | $1,861 |
| Imports | $1,400 | $2,370 | $2,532 |
| Net exports or trade gap | –$367 | –$708 | –$671 |

*Source:* Bureau of Economic Analysis, Department of Commerce (www.bea.gov).

*Note:* Exports are goods and services sold abroad. Imports are goods and services bought from abroad. Both are in billions of current dollars, annual data, no deflator. Net Exports are exports minus imports. Trade gap is imports minus exports, and is a negative number.

meant was that the Great Recession had so far not had a big effect on the rest of the world. The economic growth of the rest of the world slowed up, but did not start to fall. This continued flow of money into the United States for exports helped cushion the U.S. recession.

Then, in the fourth quarter of 2008, both the American economy and the economy of the rest of the world fell off the edge of the cliff together. At that point the loss of demand in all the major countries started to reverberate back and forth. Lack of demand for American exports must mean less income for Americans. If Americans have less income, then they have less demand for imports from the rest of the world. If, on the other hand, Americans demand less from the rest of the world, then the rest of the world has less income. If the rest of the world has less income, it will demand fewer American exports.

This reverberation effect around the world reduced the exports of all countries and aided the vicious circle downward for all economies. One lesson is that any policy to end the Great Recession of 2007 to 2009 must include a unified world policy from all countries. They only have to agree on what policy, which they have not done at the time this was written.

The final question is how the divergent growth of exports and of imports affected the trade deficit in the expansion of 2001 to 2007. In the expansion, American imports once again rose faster than exports, raising the trade deficit as the gap increased. This fact is presented in a simple table, Table 10.1.

The table shows that in 2001, President Bush's first year in office and a recession year, the trade gap was $367 billion. This meant that imports were that much higher than exports, so net exports were negative and there was a trade deficit.

By the end of the expansion in 2007, the trade deficit had grown to $708 billion. In other words, imports had grown much faster than exports, so the trade gap increased and far more money flowed out of the United States. This was one factor leading to the Great Recession of 2007 to 2009.

Europeans and Asians during the expansion could congratulate themselves that they outcompeted the United States. They could also claim that the Great Recession of 2007 to 2009 began in the United States, partly because of the increasing trade deficit.

On the other hand, the American Great Recession beginning in 2007 had spread to all parts of the world by the fourth quarter of 2008. So the global economy had a drastic fall. Then the trade of every country in the global economy declined. Decline in each country reverberated to all the others, being one major factor resulting in the ever-deeper vicious circle downward. In the first quarter of 2009, both the European and Japanese economies declined at double-digit annual rates.

**Imports of Raw Materials**

Imports of raw materials pose special problems for American business. A very large portion of all raw materials used in America is produced abroad and imported by American business. Suppose the price of raw materials from abroad, such as the price of oil from Venezuela or tin from Bolivia, rises in an expansion more rapidly than the price of consumer goods in the United States. Suppose an American company produces tin cans and the price of tin cans has been constant. Now suppose the price of tin in the world market goes up. The U.S. company will have lower profits per can. Figure 10.7 shows what actually happened to the price of raw materials in relation to the price of consumer goods over the average of the five business cycles from 1970 to 2001. Figure 10.7 shows that the ratio of raw material prices to consumer goods prices declined slowly at the beginning of an expansion. After the midpoint of the expansion, however, the ratio of raw material prices to the consumer price index (CPI) rose rapidly to the cycle peak.

Why did this important ratio decline in the early recovery? As the expansion began, consumer prices always began a slow rise due to the higher demand for goods and services. On the other hand, raw material prices were still very low, due to the previous recession. Since raw material prices remained low while consumer prices were rising, the result was that the price ratio of materials to consumer prices had to decline. In the recovery in these five cycles, American producers of consumer goods and services were helped by the low price of raw materials (mostly imported). The relatively lower costs helped raise their profits.

Raw material prices rose more rapidly than consumer prices in the last half of the average expansion. The reason is that production of finished goods can rise rapidly when more goods are needed. Production of additional raw materials takes time. Raw materials are not made in a factory, but must be

Figure 10.7 **Ratio of Crude Material Prices to Consumer Prices by Cycle, 1970–2001**

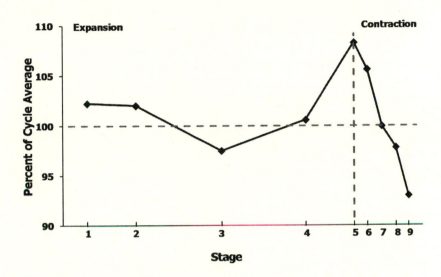

*Source:* Bureau of Labor Statistics, series WPSSOP1000 and CUSR0000SA0 (www.bls.gov).

*Note:* Price of crude materials is an index of the price of raw materials and semifinished materials. Consumer prices are defined as the consumer price index of all urban consumers. Both series are seasonally adjusted monthly data, aggregated to quarterly data.

either mined or planted and harvested. Therefore, when more raw materials are demanded, there is often a shortage before additional materials can be produced. As a result, the price of raw materials will rise. This behavior often causes the price of raw materials to rise faster than the price of consumer goods and services.

In late expansion, American profits are hurt more and more by this relatively rapid increase in the price of raw materials.

On the other hand, in each recession, raw material prices fell much faster than consumer prices. The reason is that the output of agricultural raw materials cannot be reduced in a day. Moreover, an idle mine still must be guarded and maintained. Thus, for a while after the recession began, producers still had additional supplies to sell. Raw material prices had to therefore fall rapidly in the recession or Great Recession.

Low raw material prices helped American companies who produce consumer goods from raw materials bought abroad during the average recession. For this reason, the profits of American business did not decline as fast in a recession as they otherwise would.

141

One very important raw material is oil. The limited amount of oil in the world and the fact that it takes millions of years to create more has caused sharp competition for supplies and vast disruption worldwide when the supply is reduced for any reason. Sometimes, the biggest oil producers cut back the supply in a coordinated effort to force the price higher. If the market for oil contracts, the price then declines suddenly.

The problem of sudden shifts in oil prices hit the American consumer a hard blow at the end of the expansion of 2001 to 2007. Oil prices went higher and higher. Some people had to choose between spending money for food and spending it to use their cars to go to work.

When the Great Recession of 2007 to 2009 became serious, oil prices declined rapidly. This decline helped most American corporations, but not enough to overcome the Great Recession.

Figure 10.8 compares the ratio of raw material prices to consumer prices for the average of the five cycles from 1970 to 2001 with the behavior of that ratio in the Bush cycle of 2001 to 2009. Figure 10.8 demonstrates that the average behavior of the previous cycles was repeated generally in the Bush cycle of 2001 to 2009 (with data only up to the end of 2008).

The movements in the Bush cycle, however, were far sharper and clearer. In the average of the previous five cycles, the ratio moved very little in most of the expansion, though it did rise in the last stage of the expansion. During the whole expansion of the Bush cycle, the ratio of crude material prices to consumer prices rose significantly. (The term *crude materials* is used in government data, but this chapter will use the more popular term *raw materials*.)

During the average recession of the five cycles, the ratio of raw materials to consumer prices fell moderately. In the Great Recession under President Bush, however, the ratio rose in the first stage of the recession, Then, as the crisis deepened, the ratio fell very, very fast for the rest of the Great Recession to date.

What does this all mean? The rise during the whole expansion is for the usual reasons. Raw material prices rise rapidly because of the strong demand for them from the whole developed capitalist world, but the supply takes time to increase, so prices must rise.

The spectacular increase of the ratio just after the cycle peak reflects a very interesting fact. American consumer prices became stagnant in the Great Recession, and then began to fall. The rest of the world, however, was not yet in a recession. So the global price of raw materials continued to rise. Since the global price of raw materials was rising rapidly, while U.S. consumer prices were fairly flat, the ratio of one to the other had to rise.

In the rest of the Great Recession to the end of 2008, the world market was feeling the Great Recession. Therefore, following the usual pattern, raw

Figure 10.8 **Ratio of Crude Material Prices to Consumer Prices by Cycle, 1970–2001 and 2001–2008**

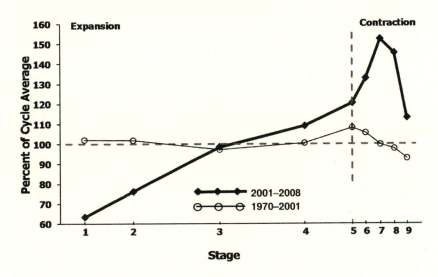

*Source:* Bureau of Labor Statistics, series WPSSOP1000 and CUSR0000SA0 (www.bls.gov).

*Note:* Price of crude materials is an index of the price of raw materials and semifinished materials. Consumer prices are defined as the consumer price index of all urban consumers. Both series are seasonally adjusted monthly data, aggregated to quarterly data. Also note that the cycle goes to 2009, but the available data went only to the fourth quarter of 2008.

material prices fell much faster than U.S. consumer prices. Because some raw material prices had risen in a bubble, they fell drastically when the bubble was deflated.

In summary, the expansion of 2001 to 2007 showed that the rise of raw material prices in the expansion hurt American profits. The fast fall of raw material prices in the Great Recession helped to support U.S. profits against an even stronger decline.

**How Recession Spreads in the Global Economy**

Recessions and depressions spread through the global economy by three different mechanisms: trade, investment, and finance.

The first mechanism is trade. When a recession in the United States reduces American imports, it hurts the trade of other countries and reduces their profits and their employee income. The other country in turn will reduce its imports and this hurts the rest of the world, including the United States. This

143

reverberation goes around the world, making trade worse and worse. The reverberation effect in trade was discussed in detail above.

It was shown above that this mechanism operated at top speed in the Great Recession and financial crisis of 2008. American production led the way downward, so American imports started falling soon after the beginning of the recession. For a little while, it looked like other countries might be able to skip the U.S. recession. American imports, however, provide a big money inflow to many other countries. So these countries soon found their exports dropping and money from trade with America disappearing. As they went into the Great Recession for this and other reasons, their own imports declined, which meant that the United States could export that much less to them.

A second mechanism to spread recessions is the investment process. When American business no longer sees profit ahead, it reduces its investment in the expansion of U.S. industry. On the other hand, the Great Recession in the United States not only reduces the profit of American investors, but also reduces the profit of those foreign investors who had previously invested from abroad in the United States. With less profit, they have less to invest in their own country.

Investment not only relies on objective estimates of future conditions, but also is always overpessimistic or overoptimistic. A poor profit outlook in America may cause a major convulsion in the U.S. stock market. In the modern world, the pessimism spreads immediately to the rest of the world. So all stock exchanges follow the first one to make a big move up or down.

A full-scale discussion of foreign investment in each country of the global economy would require a discussion of the imperialism and colonialism of the nineteenth and twentieth centuries, the very rapid increase in foreign investment since the 1970s by all the major developed countries, and the spread of a small number of giant corporations that operate within and dominate over most countries. (The process of globalization, its weaknesses and its limitations, is discussed at length in Sherman *The Business Cycle* [1991] and in some of the Selected Readings at the end of this chapter.)

Because of the entanglement of all countries in the global economy, the Great Recession of 2007 to 2009 spread from the United States to other countries in various ways. As the U.S. stock market continued to fall, foreign investors left it in droves and did not soon return. They did their best to get all their money out of American corporations. The collapse of confidence in American profits sent shudders throughout all stock markets and all forms of investment around the world. The investment panic spread, not only because of the actual decline of profits, but also because of the fear and uncertainty about the future.

In addition to the developed capitalist countries, each of which had its own growing problems even before the American recession, the underdeveloped countries often base their entire economy around trade in one or two main exports. When the United States suddenly stopped buying many raw materials, and when other developed countries also stopped buying these materials, the economies of many underdeveloped countries collapsed much further than the economies of the developed capitalist countries. People in the underdeveloped countries suffered far more terribly on the average than those in developed countries, even though people suffered plenty in the developed countries.

The third mechanism for the spread of recessions in the global economy is international finance. The international financial market operates in many ways. To give one example, the crisis in the American mortgage sector caused by too risky mortgages was spread to a number of European banks because they had bought large numbers of these mortgages when they looked like an eternal source of wealth. When the people who had taken loans against the mortgages could no longer pay back interest or principal, the banks were left holding hundreds of billions of dollars of worthless assets.

There are international transactions of trillions of dollars a day. These involve all financial corporations everywhere in the world in a close web of activity. When one goes down, the ripple spreads rapidly. As more banks fail, those others with deposits or investments in them might also fail. Again there is a vicious circle downward.

**Frightening Financial Flows**

The trade deficit itself was a drag on the American economy because it meant that many billions of dollars flowed out of the country. That outflow of dollars was counteracted by the equally immense flow of billions of dollars back into U.S. financial markets.

Those dollars flowing back into the United States propped up the economy and the expansion of 2001 to 2007. They left the U.S. economy dependent on foreign capital from China, Japan, and Europe to keep it going. Should those countries stop investing the dollars they accumulate from selling their exports in the United States and invest elsewhere, the U.S. economy would be left in shambles.

The unprecedented size of the U.S. trade deficit made these financial flows especially dangerous. By 2007, the U.S. trade deficit relative to the size of the U.S. economy had reached 6 percent of GDP. The last time prior to this decade that the U.S. trade deficit had been above 4 percent of GDP was in 1816, when British imports flooded into the United States after the end of the War of 1812.

Here is the present danger. The U.S. economy racks up a record trade deficit. Buying foreign exports increases the supply of dollars in foreign hands. At the same time, the United States must attract enough dollars from abroad to pay for the deficit in its current trade account. The deficit was more than $700 billion in 2007. In other words, the U.S. trade deficit creates the supply of dollars abroad, but that generates the U.S. need for dollars from abroad to pay for its deficit.

Dollars are lured back into the U.S. economy from overseas in two ways. Foreign investors can buy stock in U.S. corporations or they can buy government bonds from the U.S. Treasury. Because profits in the U.S. stock market were risky and uncertain throughout the Bush expansion even before collapsing in 2008, almost all the money from overseas investors came from buying U.S. corporate and Treasury bonds.

The monies to be invested in the U.S. economy can be envisioned as a giant swimming pool of savings. An increasingly large share of the water in the American savings pool now comes from abroad. When foreign capital is a substantial part of the water in the U.S. savings pool, the sheer volume of capital that can flow out of the country is much larger. This made the U.S. stock market and other asset markets more volatile.

Through much of the expansion of 2001 to 2007, foreigners were happy to purchase the gobs of debt issued by the U.S. Treasury and corporate America to cover the trade deficit. That kept U.S. interest rates low. Much of that flood of savings from abroad went into residential real estate. International buyers bought up mortgage-backed securities. This swelled the housing bubble, whose collapse contributed so mightily to the financial crisis.

**Capital Flight and the Crisis**

Global investors' stock and bond investments became overloaded with U.S. assets. By 2007, foreign investors held more than half of U.S. Treasury bonds. China alone held nearly $1.8 trillion in U.S. assets. The growing dependence of the United States economy on foreign capital was a sure warning sign of the financial crisis that soon came.

In the summer of 2007, capital flight struck. Foreign investors slashed their holdings of U.S. securities by a record amount. The dollar's value fell, declining relative to other currencies for most of a year. As it became clear that the unpaid mortgage interest would cause widespread losses for investors, large numbers of foreign investors sold their U.S. assets, intensifying the crisis. The withdrawal of foreign investors helped cause the stock market collapse as well. With the departure of foreign savings from the U.S. economy, the supply of credit for buying automobiles, for student loans, and even for corporate loans dried up, making matters worse.

Decline in each country reverberated to all the others. This process was one major factor that resulted in the ever-deeper vicious circle downward.

Then a curious thing happened. Foreign investors returned to the United States as their economies collapsed. They did not invest in the U.S. housing market or buy U.S. stocks or corporate bonds. Rather, like domestic investors, foreign investors flocked to the safest haven in the financial world, U.S. Treasury bonds.

That turnaround had two dramatic effects. First, with the return of foreign savings to the United States, the value of the dollar appreciated. That made U.S. exports more expensive and imports a bargain. As a result, the trade deficit worsened, further slowing the U.S. economy.

Second, the stampede into Treasury bonds allowed the federal government to borrow at extremely low interest rates, close to zero percent. How the government spends that money will determine the nature of the recovery that eventually emerges from the crisis.

## Clues to Remember

First, imports rose faster than exports in the expansion of 2001 to 2007 and in most previous expansions. The rise in imports led to increasing trade deficits in each expansion. The outflow of money through the trade deficit tends to lower American domestic demand profits.

This conclusion that money leaked out through the trade deficit, however, is modified by the fact that foreign money came into the United States in the form of investments, as well as loans to the U.S. government. That huge amount of money, which counteracted the U.S. trade deficit to some extent, could also become a large problem if the money flowed out again. Some of it did flow out during the financial panic of 2008, making the crisis worse. There is a worry that such an outflow could happen again.

Second, in contractions, imports go down faster than exports, so the trade deficit decreases. The decrease in the trade deficit in contractions, however, has been less than the increase in expansions in the last six U.S. business cycles. Thus, in the period since 1970, the trade deficit has tended to get larger and larger over time.

Third, raw material prices usually rise more than consumer prices in an expansion. This hurts the profits of corporations in the developed capitalist countries. It is another factor leading from prosperity to recession or depression. In recessions, prices of raw materials go way down. This decrease cushions the profits of corporations in the developed capitalist world, but it creates great suffering for the people of the underdeveloped countries.

Fourth, international investment is now closely intertwined in the global economy. So a recession or depression beginning in one country soon reduces investment in all countries.

Fifth, the international financial sector is also closely tied together. So failures of banks in one country tend to spread very rapidly around the global economy. If the U.S. economy looks too fragile at any time, a great deal of money could flow out in a short time.

It is worth emphasizing that all these mechanisms operated to spread instability around the world in the Great Recession of 2007 to 2009. So there was a worldwide Great Recession. It should also be said that these mechanisms spread the crisis only after it started in the United States. It would not have affected other countries to such an extent, however, if they were not already in a weak and fragile condition.

**Suggested Readings**

On U.S. international dominance in finance after World War II, see the excellent study by Harry Magdoff, *Imperialism Without Colonies* (2003). For a simple, but detailed discussion of trade, investment, and finance in the global economy, see Part 4 of Sherman et al., *Economics: An Introduction to Traditional and Progressive Views* (2008). For a higher-level, but older discussion of the global economy and these three sources of instability, see Sherman's *The Business Cycle: Growth and Crisis Under Capitalism* (1991), Chapter 16.

An article explaining the international financial flows in simple English is John Miller's "Dollar Anxiety," in *Dollars & Sense* (2005). Another clear article is Marie Duggan, "The Specter of Capital Flight," also in *Dollars & Sense* (2009).

# Part III

# Diagnosis and Cure of
# the Roller Coaster Economy

In Part III, the reader will find the fruit of their labor. Chapter 11 puts together the key empirical data from Part II to present a coherent story of how the Great Recession was created. Chapter 12 presents a policy for full employment and an end to the roller coaster.

# 11

# How Violent Profit Swings Cause the Roller Coaster

In order to understand the Great Recession and the financial crisis, this chapter asks and answers several key questions. How did the weak recovery of 2001 to 2003 become an economic boom with rapid growth? How did the boom become a recession? Why was the recession so deep and why did it lead to a financial crisis? What are the prospects for recovery?

## Recovery and the Virtuous Circle, 2001 to 2007

The first part of expansion after a recession is called a recovery. During the recovery early in the expansion of 2001 to 2007 the rivers of revenue flowed more rapidly, while mountains of costs were only low hills, easy to cross. Yet the lingering effects of the 2001 recession, and the lack of confidence it had caused, meant that the recovery was weak and slow for some time. The economy expanded slowly, jobs continued to decline for a while, and the stock market reached its lowest point in March 2003.

Only in 2003 did the economy finally spring to life again after the devastation of the recession. Even in the weak recovery, the total income of the whole country, called national income, was rising slowly. As consumer income rose, so did consumer spending. As consumer spending increased, it led to increases in production. More production required more employees.

The increases in wages and salaries fueled more consumer spending. By 2003 a virtuous circle began to emerge. A virtuous circle in the economy means that an increase of one economic variable leads to an increase of another, which then rebounds to spur the first variable still farther upward, with the process continuing indefinitely. This virtuous circle is found in every expansion. In the virtuous circle, more jobs and more employee income led to more demand for goods and services, which led to further expansion.

Furthermore, government spending rose with the usual help that the government gives to the economy. The Bush administration added war spending for the invasion of Iraq. This government spending continued and pushed the virtuous circle upward. Increased government spending put more people to work, generating more wages and salaries for additional purchasing power.

At the same time, the rest of the world was also recovering. Therefore, it demanded American exports. This further helped the recovery. As Americans got higher income, they also imported more from other countries. The greater demand bounced from country to country, so expansion reverberated around the world.

As the weak recovery turned into a rapid upward expansion, the rivers of spending flowed freely. Since there was plenty of revenue available, business began to spend on new investment in buildings and equipment. In this expanding economy, profits rose rapidly, but wages and salaries were slow to increase (for the reasons given in Chapter 4).

Although wages and salaries remained low for some time, most people still remembered the recession, so they were hesitant about borrowing. Because there was not much borrowing, interest rates also remained low.

Moreover, people were still unsure about their income, so they did not rush out and import a great deal from foreign countries. Therefore, relatively little money flowed out to foreign countries.

In addition, there were large piles of raw materials, so prices of raw materials on the world market remained low. Thus all the major categories of cost were low.

Since revenue was pouring in—from consumers, new business expansion, government, and foreigners—while costs remained low, it is no wonder that profits were phenomenal. The virtuous circle, it appeared, would go on and on. The economy expanded smoothly, rising higher and higher. Unfortunately, this optimism, found in every expansion on record, was only a fairy tale, as shown below.

## The Bush Expansion, 2001 to 2007 to the Great Recession

The sequence of events in the expansion was the same in the Bush cycle as in all earlier cycles, but more violent and dramatic in some respects. One startling aspect of the Bush expansion was the enormity of the gap between sluggish wages and salaries versus the amazing growth of corporate profit. The ensuing slow, but steady, decline of economic growth in the last half of the expansion was also similar to previous cycles.

In the middle of the expansion, the virtuous circle seemed to continue. Amid this growth, however, there were other trends that did not bode well for future profit. There were several disproportions and gaps that slowly developed in the economy.

The gaps appeared in every major area of the economy. There was the gap between all the output produced by employees and the amount that employees got for their services. There was the gap between all consumer goods and services at present prices and the amount of income that the population had to spend. There was the gap between the amount that government took in as revenue and the amount that government spent. There was a gap between exports and imports, called the trade deficit. Finally, there was the gap between prices of raw materials and the price of finished consumer goods. Each of these gaps will be examined below.

## The Income Gap

The benefits of the Bush expansion were distributed unequally among the American people. The national income of the United States can be divided into two very different streams. Employee income includes wages, salaries, commissions, bonuses, and benefits, such as health care. The other category is property income. Property income includes rent, interest, and profit. Profit here includes both corporate profit and the profit of individual and partnership businesses.

In the Bush expansion, employee income grew more slowly than property income. There was a growing gap between the income of employees and the value of the goods and services produced by them. So where does the rest of the money from sales go? The rest of the money from sales of the product flowed to those who owned the corporations. In the Bush expansion, there was a rising flood of interest payments, rental payments, and corporate profit. The Bush economy continued to expand, but the wealthy got most of the rewards. Thus, most of the employees of the giant corporations saw themselves getting nowhere, even though abundance appeared to be everywhere. This was the source of the growing anger seen at that time. This anger was greater during the Bush expansion than in most previous expansions because the gap grew at a far greater speed in that expansion.

## The Consumption Gap

The growing income gap created a consumption gap. When the great mass of employees received far less income than the total consumer goods and services produced, there was not enough money income to buy all the goods and services that were produced at the going price. That is called a consumption gap.

Of course, it was theoretically possible that spending by the property owners could have filled the gap. Those few rich, large property owners, including owners of corporate stock, were, however, a small minority of all consumers. Therefore, they could buy only a small percentage of all the goods and services. This was true even though each one of the large property owners bought large amounts of each item. Many property owners were very rich, so they fulfilled their consumption desires at a high level, but they still used just a small percent of each thing. For example, even a wealthy family did not buy more than a few refrigerators. Most refrigerators were being bought by millions of employees, but many employed did not have enough money for one new refrigerator.

Thus the consumer spending of wealthy property owners filled only a small percentage of the consumption gap. This still left many goods and services unsold. The unsold goods reduced profit by the end of the expansion. The unsold goods and services, such as the millions of automobiles sitting on dealers' lots, were one cause of the Great Recession.

## The Credit Balloon

Some of the consumption gap was filled by spending that did not come from income, but rather by borrowed credit. During the Bush expansion, most people in America spent an amount of credit every year equal to a significant percent of their whole income. In 2005, consumer credit was 139 percent of national income. The average person made interest payments equal to 13 percent of income to the credit agencies.

In the expansion of 2001 to 2007, credit expanded every year at the same pace as total employee income. So credit represented the gap between income and consumption. The credit gap was the amount of new credit given out each year, showing that income was insufficient to fill the needs of consumers.

Does credit do good or harm to the aggregate economy? By temporarily filling the gap between consumption goods and services marketed and the amount of consumer income, it kept the economy afloat. This credit growth did not happen only in the Bush expansion. For many years, from the 1970s until 2007, credit just kept growing in the American economy. It grew rapidly in expansions, but continued to grow slowly in most recessions. So by 2007, it was at a very high level.

Although credit kept the Bush expansion alive, it made the economy more and more fragile and liable to a credit crisis. This problem of a fragile economy, built on much credit, has been seen in every business cycle, making every recession worse. The crisis, however, has been most spectacular two times. In the Great Depression, the existence of huge amounts of credit in a credit bubble propelled the economy beyond any reasonable optimism and then helped cause a huge financial crash.

In 2007, credit had been rising for decades, with no periods of big decline, so there was a vast credit bubble. Cracks in the financial system began to appear by 2007 after amazing amounts of credit had been issued. By trading loans with each other, banks built towers of paper on top of other towers of paper. With a relatively small investment, they borrowed large amounts to make enormous profits. The first cracks in the pyramids of paper were generally ignored by the banks and the government regulators, but the cracks grew in a full-blown financial crisis and panic in 2008. Many of the largest banks, insurance companies, and other financial corporations went bankrupt, while the stock market slid 50 percent from its peak. Fortunes built on credit, smoke, and mirrors suddenly collapsed.

The reduction of employee income, along with the sudden reduction of credit, reduced sales of goods and services. This was an important factor reducing profit at the end of the expansion and the beginning of the Great Recession.

**The Rise in the Interest Rate**

One other aspect of credit caused problems late in the Bush expansion. Higher interest rates helped to push down the profit rate. As shown in Chapter 8, interest rates were low at the beginning of the expansion. They went even lower in the early expansion because more credit was available, but memories of the recession make people very hesitant to borrow.

As the expansion continued, both consumers and corporations became far more optimistic. As their borrowing increased and accelerated, the interest rate started to climb. Increasing optimism continued to boost the interest rate all the way to the cycle peak. By the end of the expansion, the larger amount of credit and the higher interest rates become a greater burden.

In the Bush expansion, by 2007 there was pressure on consumers to buy fewer goods and services on credit because of the rising interest rates. In particular, there was the very high interest charged by the credit card companies. There was even some added pressure from rising interest rates on corporations to invest less than they would otherwise have done. It was one more factor reducing profit in 2007 at the end of the Bush expansion.

**The Raw Materials Gap**

Another problem for American profit was that raw material prices rose rapidly in the last half of the Bush expansion. In the late expansion, there was a gap between the rising demand for raw materials, which rises with GDP, and the supply of raw materials, which rises more slowly. The reason that raw material production took longer to rise than industrial production was that raw materials do not increase just by speeding up a production line in a factory. Raw materials had to be dug from the ground or grown through agriculture. The gap between the supply of and demand for raw materials raised their prices at a rapid pace toward the end of the Bush expansion.

Rising raw material prices meant that American producers of finished goods (consumer and capital goods) had to pay more to the raw material producers in the rest of the world. By 2007, most raw materials came from foreign countries. The price of these imported raw materials constituted a cost for aggregate American business.

Raw material prices, such as oil, went up rapidly in the last half of Bush expansion. In fact, as shown in Chapter 10, the price of raw materials went up faster than consumer prices in the United States. So most American companies made less profit due to the higher raw material prices. For example, when the price of oil and gas rose, American Airlines made less profit. The problem at the end of the Bush expansion was that there was a gap between the price of imported raw materials and the price of the domestically produced final goods.

**Government and the Deficit Gap**

What happened to the government deficit in the expansion of 2001 to 2007? In the first half of that expansion, the rising costs of the Bush wars in Iraq and Afghanistan led to rapidly rising government spending. In addition, the Bush tax cuts for the rich reduced the flow of government taxes. The higher spending for war, combined with the cuts in taxes, produced an upsurge in deficit spending in the first half of the expansion.

In the last half of the Bush expansion, taxes rose automatically, as they always do in a boom with rising income. Government spending rose only slowly because spending on items needed in the previous recession, such as unemployment compensation, ended, and spending fell. Since taxes rose more rapidly than government spending, the amount of deficit spending fell.

What was the impact of the decline in government deficit spending in the last half of the Bush expansion? Since deficit spending puts a flow of money into the economy, the lower deficit spending put less money into the economy. Therefore, the decreasing deficit spending was another factor tending to lower profits at the end of the Bush expansion.

**The Trade Gap**

The above sections have examined demand by consumers, investors, and government. One other possible source of demand is trade with foreign countries.

Exports are those goods and services that flow out of the United States, so exports bring a flow of money into the United States. Imports are the goods and services that flow into the United States. To pay for imports, American money flows out to foreign countries.

The question is: what happened to exports and imports in the last half of the Bush expansion leading to the Great Recession? As the economy expanded, Americans had more income. They used that income partly to buy more imports. For this reason, American imports increased rapidly in the last half of the Bush expansion.

Exports, on the other hand, depend on the demand from foreign countries. If that demand does not move in exactly the same way as American import demand, it will often rise more slowly than American imports. This relatively slow rise of exports happened in the Bush expansion.

This pattern in the Bush expansion of 2001 to 2007 followed the usual pattern of the five previous cycles. Specifically, American imports rose faster than exports, so the trade gap expanded. This meant a greater net flow of money out of the country. This hurt domestic demand and therefore hurt domestic profit.

One must remember that America was already running a trade deficit for most of the years since 1970. When one says that the trade deficit grew worse, this means that money from exports fell even further below money flowing out for imports.

When the American economy started to slow and incomes declined during the recession in 2007, imports declined more than exports. Therefore, the trade deficit declined somewhat. As the world economy sank further into the Great Recession, however, exports collapsed and the trade deficit widened again.

**The Violent Ups and Downs of Profit**

The violent ups and downs of profit may be seen in Figure 11.1. The figure gives a clear picture of the usual behavior of profit. This is seen in both the latest cycle, including data from 2001 through 2008 (all that was available), and also in the average of the previous five cycles. Both periods follow the same general directions. Both go up rapidly in most of the expansion. Both decline in the stage before the cycle peak. Both decline in most of the recession. This reflects the continuance of the same basic features of capitalism.

Yet the two cycle patterns differ in the amplitude of their rise and fall. By comparison with the Bush cycle, the movements of the average of the earlier five cycles appear very tame. Profits rose far more rapidly in 2001 to 2007 than in the average expansion of the previous five cycles. Profits in the crisis of 2008 fell with breathtaking speed compared with the slower decline in the

Figure 11.1  **Corporate Profits by Cycle, 1970–2001 and 2001–2009**

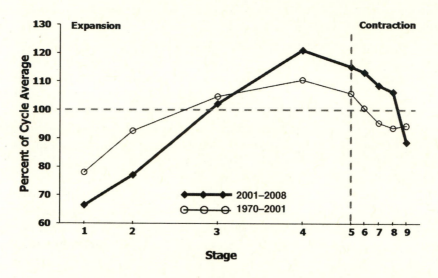

*Source:* Department of Commerce, Bureau of Economic Analysis, NIPA table 1.7.5, line 17, and NIPA table 1.1.9, line 1 (www.bea.gov).

*Note:* Profit is corporate profit before taxes. Latest cycle, 2001.4 to 2008.4, and average of five cycles, 1970.4 to 2001.4, in billions of dollars, adjusted for inflation by the gross domestic product implicit price deflator from the Department of Commerce. Seasonally adjusted quarterly data, at annual rates. Also note that the cycle goes to 2009, but the available data went only to the fourth quarter of 2008.

average of the five previous cycles. The deep decline in the Great Recession was due to the accumulated structural changes of the last three or four decades. The next part of this chapter explains why profit moved in these ways and what was its impact.

**Profit in a Nutcracker**

Remember that profit equals revenue minus costs. The sections above showed that near the end of the Bush expansion aggregate revenue was rising slowly, while aggregate costs rose rapidly. Specifically, in the last half of the Bush expansion, consumer spending growth was declining. Federal deficit spending was declining, which means less net flow of money to consumers and corporations. The trade deficit was widening, so there was more money flowing out of the United States.

On the cost side, interest payments were rising. Raw material prices (such as gas and oil) were rising rapidly. Therefore profits reach a peak a stage before the peak of expansion. Sales of goods and services were still rising slowly, but the margin of profit was already falling.

The analogy of the nutcracker helps here. From the beginning of expansion until about the midpoint of expansion, the jaws of the nutcracker were widening. Widening jaws meant that the revenue jaw was rising rapidly while the cost jaw was rising very little.

In the last half of expansion, however, the revenue jaw starts closing from above, while the cost jaw rises rapidly from below. Profit and many human hopes are lost between those awful closing jaws. Throughout most of the Great Recession, the jaws continue to close, crushing corporate profit. Of course, corporations shared the agony by firing employees.

Once profit started falling, the expansion was doomed. A fall of profit inevitably led to a fall of investment. The next section will explore the impact of the investment decline. In fact, as soon as profit started to fall, even though it was falling very slowly at first, many gaps showed a very slight tendency to close. For example, the consumer gap gets a tiny bit smaller. Unfortunately, the slight closing of the consumer gap was too late. The falling profit still acted on investment with a time lag—and that set off the Great Recession. The profit peak was the key event toward which the increasing problems of the expansion had been pointing.

**The Investment Gap**

At the end of the Bush expansion, investment followed profit like a dog on a leash. Following profit with a time lag, investment normally falls at the cycle peak. In the Great Recession, as profit slowly fell, the amount of investment continued to rise for a few quarters, but its rate of growth declined to almost nothing. Then, in the financial crisis in the fourth quarter of 2008, investment suddenly took an immense decline.

Once investment started to fall in the Great Recession, there was a growing gap between the peak level of investment and the rapid slide downward of its actual level. In the Great Recession, once investment dropped rapidly in the fourth quarter of 2008, a vicious downward spiral developed in the economy. Unemployment increased at half a million or more a month. Less employment led to less employee income, which led to less consumer spending.

Investment and current production went down hand in hand. When investment came to a halt, the whole capitalist economy, which was dynamic and based on growth, also came to a halt. The capitalist economy then began to contract.

## Crisis and the Vicious Circle

The underlying problems of the Bush expansion were the basic cause of the Great Recession. The situation leading to the crisis was forged both by the usual cyclical gaps and disproportions but also by structural changes over the last thirty years or so. In 2007, the catalyst that set off the Great Recession was a housing crisis. Because lenders had been wildly overenthusiastic about giving mortgage credit, the housing crisis became a financial panic in 2008. In the minds of most people, these events "caused" the Great Recession. These immediate causes created the crisis, however, mainly because the stage was already set by the increasing gaps in the market and by the long-run bubbles in housing and credit.

Once the Great Recession began, however, everything went bad, as in every recession to a lesser extent. Total wages and salaries went down as employment fell. Consumer spending went down because employee income went down. Moreover, because the profit outlook was bad, investment spending went down. Unemployment went up. Bankruptcies went up. House foreclosures went up.

Furthermore, this process was a cumulative spiral downward. Reduced investment meant fewer jobs. Fewer jobs meant less consumer spending. Less consumer spending led to still less investment spending. And so forth in a vicious downward spiral.

The result was that consumers and investors lost confidence. So all the objective damage to the economy was magnified by a wave of pessimism.

## Structural Changes and the Financial Crisis

The above sections have explained why the expansion of 2001 to 2007 became the Great Recession. Why, however, did it become such a large or Great Recession and why did it generate the financial crisis of 2008 to 2009? The answer lies in the change in the economic structure of the United States that built up slowly over many decades. From 1945, following World War II, to 2007, recessions were mild or medium strength. In 1929 began the Great Depression and in 2007 began a very serious recession, the Great Recession. What determines whether a recession will remain mild or will become a deep contraction including a financial crisis in it?

The answer has usually been determined by three main factors. They are housing, finance, and the economic situation of the rest of the world. This book showed that over several decades leading up to the Great Recession, the structure of the housing market weakened, the structure of finance and credit became very fragile, and the rest of the world had progressed to about the same structural situation.

The first condition for a crisis lies in the answer to the question: is housing weak or strong? As Chapter 6 illustrated, housing has a cycle that is somewhat different from the general business cycle, so it may coincide or not. As was shown in Chapter 6, since about 1970, housing had an unprecedented boom, with rising house prices for decade after decade. People came to expect that this unusual trend would continue forever. Instead, housing prices began to decline in 2006. They have declined at a rapid rate from 2006 to 2009. Housing construction also declined, putting thousands of construction workers out of work.

A second important factor determining the depth of a recession and the chance of a crisis is the strength or weakness of the financial system. In the Great Depression, a financial panic brought people running to take their money out of banks, which caused banks to go bankrupt. Bank failures hurt those dependent on the banks for credit or for their own deposits. Credit became unobtainable, so consumers could not buy more and businesses could not expand.

Similarly, the financial crisis in 2008 to 2009 threatened to make the Great Recession into a much deeper crisis. There were failures of banks, giant insurance companies, and giant brokerage firms. These failures were initially caused by the housing crisis, which drastically lowered the value of the companies' assets, often built on risky housing loans. Credit dried up. The end of easy credit hurt both consumers and business.

These issues were discussed above in the section on credit, but one point needs to be emphasized because of the decisive role it played in 2008. Banks had long known that they could make higher profits by borrowing capital and then investing that capital. This is called leveraging. It means that a bank begs, borrows, or steals additional capital beyond its own assets. If a bank can borrow ten times its own initial capital, then invest that amount at a high profit, the rate of profit on the bank's own initial investment will be very high.

In the last three decades especially, the banks had borrowed enormous sums, invested it, and made huge profits. They assumed that they would keep making high profits, so they could pay off the credit they borrowed. They were sure that a few sectors, such as housing, would always be cash cows with ever-rising profits. When the profits started to decline in the housing sector and some others, the banks suddenly found they could not pay back their loans. Either they would get government charity or they would die in bankruptcy court. This situation set off the financial crisis.

Third, a recession will be made worse or better depending on the international situation. If there is peace and brisk international trade, American exports may be increased, which may help profit. If, on the contrary, all other countries are in recession, then their imports from the United States will decrease instead of increasing. Each country that lowers its imports reduces the income of other countries. Therefore, a downward spiral of trade and income is often created across the world.

The economic structure of the rest of the world had evolved along the same fragile lines as the United States, so the U.S. financial crisis quickly became a global financial crisis.

One can argue whether the 2007 to 2009 contraction should be called a Great Recession or an ordinary recession. It is clear, however, that these three factors caused a terrible crisis in 2008. Both in the financial system and in the real economic system, in late 2008 and early 2009 there was a dramatic crisis, including a financial panic for a time. Without government intervention, many giant corporations, both financial and nonfinancial, would have gone bankrupt and the resulting depression would have lasted many years.

The combination of a slowly worsening structure in housing, in finance, and in the rest of the world did indeed lead to the crisis of 2008.

**Recession to Recovery**

The Great Recession and crisis of the Bush era were not over at the time of this writing, so it is impossible to discuss the full course of the path that may lead to recovery. Instead, this discussion is based on the average behavior that led to recovery in the previous five recessions. The mystery of the cause of recession or depression has been solved, but it is important to know how recoveries usually occur.

What factors can lead to recovery? In a recession, some factors always come into play to reduce decline and, eventually, start a recovery. As an exception, the Great Depression remained below its 1929 peak for ten long painful years until it was saved by a world war, when the government increased its demand to 40 percent of all GDP.

The average recession of the more recent five cycles continued downward in the vicious circle for some time. In that period, employee income from labor declined, but much slower than total output. The fact that employee income does not fall as fast as output means that there is some floor to the decline of spending on goods and services. Employee income declines slowly in the recession, while the profit part of national income falls rapidly.

As employee income stops falling so fast, so does consumer demand. So the consumer share of national income begins to rise. Yes, the share rises, but remember that the typical consumer is actually buying less at the store. If Janet is receiving only two-thirds as much salary as she was getting before the recession, she is not going to be any happier to know that profit is falling even faster than her salary.

In addition, government demand automatically picks up in the recession. For one thing, as unemployment rises, government must pay out more unemployment compensation. In general, government spending automatically rises to cover some of the problems of a business contraction.

Of course, the government may also decide at its discretion, under enormous public pressure, to speed up various types of its spending in order to stimulate the economy. Some administrations have done a lot of stimulus and some have done little.

Moreover, while government spending rises rapidly for both automatic and discretionary reasons, taxes do not remain unchanged. Taxes fall rapidly as income and sales fall. Since government spending is rising, while taxes and fees are falling, the net flow of money from the government into the economy must increase. In other words, the government deficit spending increases and that helps to pump up the economy.

Another eventual improvement of spending is usually found in trade behavior. The increasing trade deficit of the expansion falters and starts to decline. Thus, even though the U.S. trade deficit continues, it is lowered. Thus less money flows out of the United States and more is available to buy internally produced goods and services.

Why does this reduction of the trade deficit usually happen? The reason is that American imports decline. Imports decline because there is less national income, so both consumers and business have less income to import foreign goods and services.

American exports, however, depend on the rest of the world. How much will continue to flow into the United States from export sales depends on the economic health of the rest of the world. In mild American recessions, the rest of the world may be on a somewhat different cycle, so their purchase of American exports usually remains on a somewhat different path than American imports of foreign goods. In other words, American imports usually fall faster than American exports. This helps keep more money at home for buying American products.

At the end of a recession, cost conditions are usually very good for expanding a business or forming a new business. Wages and salaries are low, so the costs of hiring employees are at a minimum. Even when the recovery begins, there are many unemployed workers, so it is easy to hire new employees with cheap wages and salaries.

Raw material costs fall rapidly in a recession because there are heaps of unsold raw materials around. Thus, it is easy to buy cheap raw materials for production.

Banks were unable to lend money during the recession, so there was plenty of money for loans as soon as conditions looked better. The excess

DIAGNOSIS AND CURE OF THE ROLLER COASTER ECONOMY

of money that is standing idle in some liquid form has risen. Thus, when recovery comes, interest rates remain low and often continue to decline for lack of customers.

In sum, costs are falling while revenues are flattening out. In this situation, any rise in consumer demand brings prospects for very good profit. The fact that business expects to make a lot of profit at the beginning of a new economic expansion means that there is a lot of new investment in buildings and equipment. A new recovery ensues.

**The Solution to the Mystery**

This chapter has shown in detail why the expansion of 2001 to 2007 turned into the Great Recession and financial crisis. It was shown that in the expansion the income gap increased, the consumer gap increased, the credit bubble grew stupendously and then broke. Furthermore, interest rates rose, deficit spending decreased, the trade gap increased, and raw material prices increased faster than consumer prices. Therefore, business profit fell, causing investment, GDP, and employment to fall.

Every one of the behavior patterns discussed above has been shown to be the product of the economic institutions of capitalism (see Sherman 2003).

Finally, the financial crisis was the result of long-run structural changes in capitalism. These changes included the changes in the money and banking system that allowed financial corporations to leverage their capital into a huge pyramid built on a small amount of initial capital. The structural trends also included changes in industry that resulted in the weakening of labor unions and the bargaining power of all employees.

These changes were accompanied by an amazing housing bubble and housing crash. The housing crisis, as well as the changes in the banking system toward more risky loans, led to an equally amazing credit bubble and credit crash. Since the same trends occurred in most countries around the world, the Great Recession and financial crisis became worldwide. The problems of each country reverberated to harm the others.

**Suggested Reading**

For economists who would prefer a full model of the business cycle with statistical testing and mathematical equations with a cyclical solution, see Howard Sherman's *The Business Cycle: Growth and Crisis Under Capitalism* (1991).

**Appendix: A Simple Theory for Teaching Purposes**

This chapter found that in every expansion:

- Growing investment leads to a growing GDP.
- Growing GDP leads to certain patterns of growth in revenues and in costs.
- By the end of expansion, aggregate cost is growing faster than aggregate revenue, so business profit falls.
- Falling profit leads to falling investment.

The chapter also shows that in every recession:

- Falling investment leads to a falling GDP.
- Falling GDP leads to certain patterns of decline in revenues and in costs.
- By the end of the recession, aggregate cost is falling faster than aggregate revenue, so business profit rises.
- Rising profit leads to rising investment.

The four processes in expansion and the four processes in recession stated above can be generalized into four propositions that always hold because they reflect basic economic institutions:

- Investment determines GDP.
- GDP leads to certain patterns in revenues and in costs.
- Aggregate cost and aggregate revenue determine business profit.
- Profit determines investment, with a time lag.

These four propositions provide a framework for a theory of the business cycle. Of course, there must be additional relationships to show how long-run structural changes in the economy determine the rapidity of growth in expansions and the depth and duration of recessions.

# 12

# The Public Option for Health and Jobs

## How Democratization Can End the Business Cycle

After examining Obama's actions to end the crisis and recession, the next issue explored is Obama's proposal for a public option in health care. This chapter then turns to the ways that democratization in the economy can help to stabilize it, followed by an explanation of the proposal for a public option in jobs that could ensure permanent full employment.

### The Obama Stimulus Spending

How did the Obama administration deal with the deep recession and financial panic that it faced when it started its term? It took a number of actions, beginning with stimulus spending. It produced both a stimulus package and a new budget designed to put government spending above taxes, so as to put money into the economy.

The money was to be spent in four main areas: roads and bridges, energy designed to be clean and green, education, and health care. The spending in these areas was designed to create a stimulus based on deficit spending. Deficit spending means that the government spends more than it takes in as taxes. If the government spends only as much as it takes away in taxes, there is no stimulus to the economy. Only deficit spending necessarily stimulates the economy by putting a new flow of money into the economy. If the government receives $70 billion in taxes from people, but spends $100 billion, then the stimulus is $30 billion.

In general, deficit spending is very helpful to the economy when there is unemployment and no inflation, as in the recent Great Recession. The large amount of deficit spending over several years should help the recovery to be stronger than it otherwise would have been.

There are two main problems with deficit spending. First, if it is in an inflationary situation, it will increase inflation. That is not a problem in an economy still trying to emerge from recession. The second problem is that the deficit increases the national debt, so it increases inequality. The increased inequality is due to the fact that the bonds for the national debt are all held by the wealthy, to whom the government must pay interest.

The effects of taxation and spending depend, not just on the totals, but also on who gets taxed and where the money is spent. In the stimulus package plus the Obama budget, taxes are reduced for most people in the country, but taxes are increased for those with incomes over $250,000. From the viewpoint of consumer spending, this is very good because the average American will spend more money per dollar of income for consumption than the rich will spend on consumption per dollar of income.

**Strengths and Weaknesses of the Obama Stimulus Spending**

The Obama administration's stimulus plan and first budget focused their tax cuts on the poor and middle-income taxpayers. These measures increased taxes on the rich. This is a very good tax policy for short run stimulation because the poor and middle income groups will spend a far higher percentage of the tax cut on consumer spending than the rich would have done (see Chapter 5).

These measures promoted four main areas of spending: (1) infrastructure, such as roads and bridges; (2) energy, such as alternative, non-polluting types; (3) education, such as school construction and teachers' salaries; and (4) health care, including hospital construction and nurses' salaries. Spending on those four areas should have good effects both on short-run job growth and on long-run economic growth.

Finally, the total amount spent for these laws will be quite large relative to GDP by the time it is all spent in several years. It should therefore have a very considerable effect on the recovery.

The biggest problem was that the stimulus package had a very small immediate effect on employment. As a result, unemployment in June 2009 rose to 9.5 percent by the usual official numbers in the narrowest definition used by the U.S. Labor Department. The Labor Department, however, also publishes a broader definition of unemployment (which it calls U-6). That broader definition (U-6) includes part-time workers, who want full time work, but are unable to find it. The broader definition (U-6) also includes so-called discouraged workers, who have been looking unsuccessfully for work for months, but gave up looking in the last month. The official, narrow definition did not include these two groups. By the broader definition (U-6), the unemployment rate had risen to 16 percent by June 2009. That 16 percent of the population was subjected to a terrible experience.

This pattern of too late spending to help immediate employment has existed in every case where the U.S. government has tried to stimulate the economy and jobs. The reasons for time lags include slow congressional action, planning and engineering new projects, getting the money to the state governments, getting the state governments to move quickly, and getting the money actually spent in multi-year projects.

The Obama stimulus plan was better in many ways than in other administrations, but it still caused much human misery in unemployment. A very different structure that would result in almost instantaneous expenditure on new projects as required for jobs is discussed below in terms of the public option to guarantee full employment.

**The Public Option for Health Care**

Expenditures for health care were an important part of the Obama stimulus package and his first budget. Health care spending stimulates the economy. Hospitals require construction workers initially, but also they require doctors and nurses. Better health care allows people to live longer and better lives, but also it allows the economy to grow faster because employees are off work less for sickness.

President Obama observed that the present American health care system—mostly controlled by private insurance companies—is broken and must be fixed. An important part of the Obama plan was that everyone should have the right to use a public health plan if the private insurance plans were too expensive.

President Obama proposed and Congress passed a universal health care plan. In addition to private insurance, there is to be a public health care plan, which may be chosen by anyone who has no insurance. If this is passed, it means that the 30 to 40 million people without health insurance could get a fairly low-cost plan, with subsidies to those who need them.

If this plan becomes law, it will greatly lower costs. Plans under private insurance have administrative costs that average about 30 percent of their total costs. These administrative costs include vast amounts of complex procedures to protect their profits, as well as the high profits themselves. Non-profit and public plans, including Medicare in the United States, have administrative costs closer to 3 or 4 percent. Therefore, people choosing the public plan will have far less costs per person. These low costs will also reduce the total costs of government per person, especially since they will greatly reduce the use of expensive emergency rooms.

The United States has the most expensive health care system in the world. The next most expensive system costs only half as much. The public systems of Canada and much of Europe average less than half as much. Yet the United States gives the least care of any industrialized country. Over 30 million Americans have no health insurance. On the contrary, each of the public health care systems is universal in coverage. Therefore, the United States must solve the twin problems of lowering cost per person and making coverage universal.

The private companies are too expensive for most of the uninsured. They also prohibit many of the uninsured for various discriminatory reasons, such as a pre-existing medical problem. Therefore, the only way to insure the uninsured is to have a public option.

Furthermore, the yearly cost of public health care is far less than the yearly cost of the Iraq and Afghan wars. Suppose the Iraq war is ended and the troops are withdrawn. Suppose the Afghanistan war is ended and the troops are withdrawn. Suppose that military spending is reduced accordingly. Then there will be plenty of money to pay for the public health care system three times over. This budgetary transfer would save many lives.

Finally, it must be recognized that in reality the private insurance companies have spent extremely large amounts of money to defeat the public option for health care. The reason is that they stand to lose billions of dollars if the public plan becomes a competitor. To protect their profits, the insurance companies and their paid defenders have told an amazing number of outright lies.

Two of the lies were discussed in detail in Chapter 9: that death panels would decide whom to save or kill and that much money would go to illegal immigrants. Another falsehood designed to scare people was that women with breast cancer would have to wait many years to get an operation—another lie. The issues of health care are so threatening to the profits of the giant health insurance corporations that large amounts of money were devoted to the propaganda war, with little interest in truth.

**The Great Money Give-Away to the Financial System:**
**Absolutely Necessary or Corporate Socialism?**

The Bush administration and the Obama administration gave trillions of dollars to banks and other corporations to prevent their bankruptcy. Was this theft and corruption on a huge scale or was it a very good and necessary action? If the goal was to preserve the present economic system, then it was a very good action. It was not, however, the only way to prevent collapse if changes in the financial structure were to be considered.

Without this injection of money, the financial system would have collapsed. If the financial system collapsed, the whole economy would have collapsed. It was definitely necessary to do something.

Some critics have argued that this transfer from the taxpayers to the biggest banks may be considered the greatest theft of money in the history of the world. It is true that the money was transferred, but this view ignores the fact that the collapse of the economic system would have meant a great deal of pain for everyone over a long period of time.

The problem is that the economy has the financial system as its foundation. The financial system reaches everywhere. If apartment-dwellers want to buy a house, they go to the financial system. If a corporation wants to build a new factory, it goes to the financial system. If all the banks were allowed to fail, then the consumer would have no credit to buy food, let alone cars or homes. Corporations generally pay their employees using an intricate loan system from the banks. In other words, if the financial system stopped working for a month, the whole economy would shut down to a very large extent.

No one wants to repeat the experience of the Great Depression, when all the banks were closed for a while. There are only two choices. Save the banks in their present institutional form or drastically change the system. The Obama administration and the Democratic Congress were elected by a movement of millions of people actively seeking reforms to change the system so as to improve it. The president and the majority of Congress obviously do believe in reform, but also they want to preserve the main institutions of the economic system. They were not elected to drastically change the basic economic system. What they did saved the system, but increased inequality because some of the money will never be returned to the taxpayer.

The Obama administration's measures helped to end an immediate financial crisis, which would have ruined the economy. The problem is that these rescue measures will not prevent future recessions and depressions.

Other critics agree that the money given to the banks prevented collapse, but they still believe it was not done correctly and will have dangerous consequences. The argument is made that this is a system of corporate socialism. Corporate socialism means that the big corporations will make any profit they can in expansion, but the government will step in and save them in the following recession and crisis. This means that the big corporations are free to make billions during expansions. If they fail in a crisis, however, they will be rescued. Since the large financial corporations are smart folk who know these facts, the corporate executives will make riskier and riskier deals. They know they will be saved. Therefore, they will be greedy risk-takers and will get into even deeper trouble the next time. The economy will be ready for a new economic contraction.

The Obama administration was aware of this problem. Its answer is the proposal of new regulations. Strong financial regulations will, they believe, prevent the banks, as well as all other corporations that provide financial services, from doing anything too risky.

**Financial Reform: Regulation Versus Deregulation**

There were very few regulations of business or finance until the Great Depression in the 1930s. There were almost no rules for the stock market, the banks, the polluting corporations, the corporations that discriminated against women and against minorities, the corporations that forced people to work twelve hours a day for low pay, and the financial manipulators who built great financial pyramids on the basis of a tiny starting company.

This lack of regulation made the Great Depression worse and led to a widespread reform movement. The Roosevelt administration added regulations in all these areas and also provided employees a safety net for the first time. The safety net included retirement pensions in the form of Social Security, unemployment compensation, and insurance on bank deposits.

By the 1970s, as people forgot the agony of the Great Depression and the wild excess of the financial corporations that worsened it, conservative economists and politicians began a successful campaign to eliminate Roosevelt's financial regulations, industrial regulations, and the safety net. They claimed that the present economic institutions were self-regulating, so they always came back to a balance of supply and demand at full employment. According to conservatives, government regulations had tied the hands of private business, preventing growth and leading to recession.

As one president after another reduced financial regulations, by 2007 there were no regulations to stop unscrupulous and unsustainable schemes for making money. These included the large, legally passable schemes of giant firms such as Citicorp and AIG to make money in very risky and unsustainable ventures. These ventures made the financial sector fragile and vulnerable to crisis if the economy faltered. The economy, including housing, faltered in 2008, so the financial system crashed in 2008 and almost collapsed.

It is worth noting that almost all economists and politicians attacked financial regulations for decades, but some changed their mind in the financial crisis. For example, Senator John McCain, the Republican candidate for president in 2008, had spent several decades attacking regulations. Then, in the 2008 campaign during the financial crisis, he vigorously argued for more regulation. Then, by mid-2009, he was already back to an attack on the proposals for new regulations by President Obama.

The Obama proposal for extensive financial regulations attempted to curb the practices of the financial firms in order to ensure stability. This plan, announced in June 2009, would establish a system of government monitoring and control of all financial corporations, not just the banks. The monitors would decide if a corporation was getting into trouble with unjustified risks. The Federal Reserve System would then move in to demand that the firm get more capital assets before it made more loans and take other measures to ensure against bankruptcy. The strongest Obama proposal allowed the government to seize a financial corporation that was close to bankruptcy in order to prevent large-scale disruption. This would be a powerful tool if it survives the attempts by the banks to prevent its passage and if it were stringently enforced.

One problem with the proposal is the reliance on many different regulatory agencies for different aspects of control. This is likely to mean administrative conflict and muddle. Another administrative problem is that Congress is under heavy pressure from the immense power of the banks to soften the regulations. A third problem is that the regulators, such as the Federal Reserve System, are usually strongly influenced by the immense economic and political power of the financial corporations.

Suppose that all these obstacles are overcome and there is a strong set of financial regulations that are strictly enforced. The most that financial regulations can do is to prevent the banks and other financial corporations from making loans too far beyond their capital, loans that customers cannot pay, and acquiring other bad assets. This may prevent an extreme financial crisis or panic. It does nothing, however, to resolve the deeper economic issues that reduce corporate profit and make corporations unwilling to borrow for new investment.

The Obama plans for stimulus, temporary control of the largest corporations, and financial regulations are helpful in the short run. In order to prevent another, and possibly worse, recession after some years, however, some alternative structural solutions must be considered.

**The Alternative Structure: Democratization**

One must agree with the Obama administration that something drastic had to be done to save the economy. It will be argued, however, that there were alternatives that would have helped the economy more and also built a future without recessions and financial crises. What if the United States could find a way to continue and deepen the Obama administration's control of the major corporations in such a way as to prevent recessions by democratization of the economy?

Democratization may be contrasted with privatization. Privatization is the process of removing functions of government and putting them into private hands. Conservatives argue that privatization would lead to a more efficient and stable economy because government hampers private enterprise, is inefficient, and its actions cause instability. This process of privatization has continued for decades, producing less government activity and more private activity for profit, even in running some prisons and schools. The greater area and freedom of private enterprise in finance and industry, however, has led to the Great Recession and financial crisis.

Democratization, on the contrary, is defined as an increase in the democratic control of the economy. A more democratic economy has progressed in two main directions. One is cooperative ownership and management of enterprises by employees or by consumers. The other is ownership and management by democratically elected local, state, or federal governments. The two forms can also be combined to some degree.

Economic textbooks in the United States speak as if all enterprises are private and competitive. Actually, most are private, but most of the economy is composed of giant corporations that do not compete in the old ways. They have considerable power over prices and they make billions of dollars of profit from control of the market at prices above what they would if there were only competitive businesses.

Every American sees the power of these giant corporations in the economy every day. Every American has heard the media report for the last two years about how these giant corporations helped make the present economic mess. This book has shown in detail how the economic structure of capitalism has operated through the corporations to bring recurrent recessions, crises, and unemployment.

## Democratization Through Cooperatives

There has long been a cooperative movement in the United States. There have been enterprises based on employee control of the enterprise through a democratic mechanism. Employee ownership means a greater equality of income in the enterprise. It also means a greater incentive for employees to make innovative proposals and contribute more willingly to the enterprise. It changes the atmosphere from one of dictatorship from above to control from below through elected officers of the enterprise. This cooperative form has existed at times in many enterprises, including Hertz rental cars and United Airlines.

There have also been consumer-owned enterprises. The reason has often been to ensure delivery of important services to isolated areas or to ensure

reasonable prices. The most important single example of consumer cooperatives began in the 1930s, when it was discovered that private electric firms
refused to deliver energy to almost all rural areas because they did not consider it profitable enough. President Roosevelt and the Democratic Congress
founded what is now called the National Rural Electric Cooperative Association. This association has formed rural cooperatives to buy (and sometimes
produce) electricity at the lowest rate. Each cooperative must be democratic
and nonprofit. In 2007, there were over 900 rural electric cooperatives, located
in forty-seven states, serving over 40 million customers.

## A Cooperative Reform by President Obama

The Obama administration was forced to take over some large industrial
corporations in the crisis to prevent their disappearance through bankruptcy.
One was the Chrysler automobile company. In June 2009 it emerged from
bankruptcy. Its new common stock was owned 57 percent by the pension
fund unit of the United Auto Workers (UAW). The Fiat corporation owned
40 percent and the U.S. and Canadian governments owned the rest.

This is a combination of different forms, but the dominant ownership by
the UAW union is one type of cooperative. Workers vote democratically to
elect the officers of the UAW. So Chrysler is now to some extent a democratic
cooperative.

As pointed out above, cooperatives have many attractive features from
a democratic point of view. Cooperatives, however, make as much use of
the market as private capitalist firms, so they suffer from the same kind of
instability. Although cooperatives alone could not stop the business cycle,
employees and consumers can participate in various ways in democratic
government enterprises. Therefore, some elements of cooperation can be
combined with government ownership. Nevertheless, although cooperatives
have many attractive features, they cannot stop the cycle of boom and bust,
or the repetitive episodes of mass unemployment, so they are not discussed
further here.

## Democratization Through Public Ownership

Conservatives argue that there is no viable alternative to private, capitalist enterprise. This assertion, however, is false. Not only is 10 percent of the economy
based on cooperative or nonprofit enterprise, but there is also the public sector.
The public form of democratic ownership and control is the public enterprise,
set up by a democratically elected local, state, or federal government. Many
examples of government enterprises, shown below, have proven equally or

more efficient than the giant corporations, which do not operate under the laws of competition and are often inefficient.

An example of democratic ownership, or economic democracy, at the local level is the Los Angeles Department of Water and Power. It produces and sells water and power to all of Los Angeles. When in 2000 to 2003 California had a crisis with a shortage of electric power, two privately owned electric companies were close to bankruptcy and could not deliver enough electricity. The Los Angeles Department of Water and Power, however, not only met its obligations, but also sold additional electricity to those who needed it.

Another use of local economic democracy is the public elementary and high school. Public schools are usually run by localities with some input of money and guidance from states. Public universities are run by states. Most roads and bridges are built by states.

At the regional or state level, an interesting example is in North Dakota. In that state, there was a period of control by the populist movement of angry farmers in the late nineteenth and early twentieth centuries. North Dakota decided that control of the financial system was too important to leave to private, capitalist enterprise. Farmers and small businesses needed loans with low interest rates, and the banks were unwilling to provide them. The state of North Dakota set up the Bank of North Dakota, which was wholly state-owned and state-controlled. It still exists today and continues "to encourage and promote agriculture, commerce and industry" in North Dakota.

At the federal level, an important example is the Tennessee Valley Authority (TVA). In the 1930s, Tennessee had floods caused by uncontrolled rivers and had a shortage of reasonably priced electricity. President Roosevelt proposed the TVA both because it was needed in the long run and because it could stimulate the economy in the Great Depression. The electric companies and the Republicans opposed the legislation, but it was passed anyway. The TVA constructed dams to tame the rivers and to produce electricity. Its cheap electric power helped people to light their homes and helped Tennessee to develop. Even though its rates for sale of electricity are lower than those of the private sector, it delivers a profit to the federal budget every year.

## The Obama Administration's Temporary Control of Banking

The Obama administration was forced to take over control of most large banks in early 2009. At that point, it had an opportunity to extend democratic control over these banks indefinitely. Its intention, however, was to leave the day-to-day control to the bankers. It also wished to exit from banking as soon as possible. In June 2009, many large banks pressured the administration to give up its control over them. In fact, these banks were allowed to pay back the government loans and exit from the program. They will now revert to their old risky ways to make maximum profits, knowing that the government will always bail them out of trouble.

The government retains large blocks of stock ownership in Bank of America, Citicorp, and the largest insurance company, AIG. Once again, the government is leaving direct control of the businesses to the corporate executives. It is also intending to restore these companies to private ownership as soon as possible.

## Permanent Control of Banking

Suppose the government retained control of all the largest banks, as well as the insurance giant AIG, which also plays a major role in finance. With control of these financial giants, the government could surely stop any possibility of a new financial crisis ever arising. With direct government control, everyone would know that the largest banks could not go bankrupt, so there would be no basis for a financial crisis.

What is the difference between public ownership of the biggest banks and private ownership of these banks? Private owners always exert pressure on the chief executive officer (CEO) to make maximum profit. This means, as the years go by and the economy slows a little in late expansion, that the CEOs of private banks must take riskier and riskier chances. Then, as a recession sets in, it is their duty to the stockholders to restrict credit. Practically overnight, banks often go from offering a loan to almost anyone to offering a loan to no one. This is a major factor in worsening every recession, even if there is no financial crisis.

The behavior of a publicly appointed CEO would be different. In the boom at the end of an expansion, the bank would not issue risky credit. It would have no motive for giving consumer credit or mortgage credit to people who clearly could not pay it back. Its instructions would be to keep the boom going by giving credit to people and corporations with a good credit rating. The public bank would not take the kind of risks that led to the financial crisis.

In a recession and in the following recovery, the public banks would give as much credit as possible to anyone or any corporation with a good credit record. Thus, in a recession, as private banks were cutting back on credit, the government-owned bank would deliberately increase it.

Public ownership of the largest banks might not prevent a recession if most corporations saw no future profit and did not want to borrow. It would, however, clearly prevent a financial crisis because of the public control of lending.

176

## President Obama's Temporary Control of General Motors

In the financial crisis of 2008 to 2009, the government took temporary control in the crisis of General Motors (GM), once the country's largest nonfinancial corporation. After GM emerged from bankruptcy court, the federal government retained 60 percent of the stock.

The intention of President Obama is to have no role for government in day-to-day activities of General Motors. It is also the intention of the administration to sell its stock when the opportunity presents itself and GM's recovery is clearly under way.

If GM goes back to private ownership, then the CEO would be under pressure to maximize profits. This means that GM will borrow all the money that it can borrow in order to expand its business as fast as possible. Why not take every risk? GM knows the government will step in and bail it out if there is any problem. GM will fight to hold down wages and salaries as far as possible. It will fight against all attempts to reduce pollution or produce less-polluting cars. In short, it will do business as usual. Business as usual by all the large corporations brought on the Great Recession and financial crisis.

## General Motors and Stabilization

Now suppose that the government keeps majority control of GM. It instructs the CEO to take every possible measure to avoid crises, avoid pollution, and make long-run profit for the American taxpayer. When a recession threatens, a publicly owned GM could increase employment instead of lowering it. It could increase research activity by hiring a great many engineers. It could take new models from the drawing boards and begin construction on models with the latest technology. This would require many new workers.

GM could also hire the best-qualified engineers and scientists to produce models of environmentally safe cars. This work would also require many more workers to produce models. The new employees could work on more ways to reduce pollution and improve energy use. Because the company's long-run approach would eventually make more profit than the shortsighted attempts of private producers to maximize profits immediately, it would make profits for the American taxpayer as it helped stabilize the economy.

How many giant corporations might be publicly owned for use in stabilization? Some economists defended the flood of government money to the biggest corporations by saying that they were "too big to fail." They were too big to fail because their failure would endanger the whole economy.

Under this criterion, whenever a giant corporation is ready to fail and is "too big to fail" in the future, the government should take complete control.

177

The corporate owners should pay the price of competitive failure. The government should use only the money necessary to restore the new public corporation to a healthy state with its labor force still having jobs. The government would act only in the case of failure of the private giants. The more such large corporations the government is forced to take over and run, the more stable will be the economy.

Conservatives argue that all private enterprise is efficient and all government enterprise is inefficient. Could any government-appointed CEO, however, behave more foolishly in financial decisions than the large banks, insurance companies, Chrysler, and GM in their haste to make profits by the riskiest means? On the contrary, the examples in earlier sections make it abundantly clear that democratically owned enterprises can be very efficient and can exist for a long time.

## The Public Option for Jobs

President Obama's stimulus package had many good features, but it did not provide many immediate jobs. Just as President Obama proposed a public option for health care, there must also be a public option for jobs if there is to be rapid recovery of employment and permanent full employment in the future.

A public option for jobs means that anyone who cannot get a private job is guaranteed the option of a public job. Exactly how would this be done? Only the principles can be discussed here. The details of such plans have been discussed in a large literature: for example, Palley (2001), Sawyer (2003), and Wray (1997).

This is not a new idea in U.S. history. In the Great Depression, President Franklin Roosevelt used several different new agencies to directly employ hundreds of thousands of men and women for important projects. In the 1970s Senator Hubert Humphrey and Representative Augustus Hawkins proposed a bill for actions to ensure full employment of all employees. Their bill was so weakened by the time it passed that it only required various reports and no actions. The enormous power of the large corporations has been used to attack any proposal for a public option to maintain full employment.

As this writing, the United States has over 16 percent unemployment, including both full-time and part-time unemployment. In this situation, perhaps the simplest approach would be that a person goes to the employment office and they direct her or him to one of the following agencies, according to the area for which the person is best qualified. Employment is immediate when they show up for the new job.

The organization for one area of the public sector might be called AmeriBuild. This agency would give people jobs to improve the infrastructure, such as building bridges and roads. The jobs would vary, according to qualifications, from unskilled to engineer or manager. The jobs could be given directly by the federal government or by assignment to a similar state organization if the state is prepared to start immediately.

Building infrastructure affects the environment. Therefore, this agency might also be the place for employment on improving the environment or for conservation projects. Alternately, a separate agency for conservation work might be included.

A second public agency would be AmeriCare. It would assign people to work in the public health care system. Since health care produces 16 percent of the gross domestic product, providing qualified people for a growing public health care system would be a major source of employment.

A third public area would be run by AmeriPower. This would include traditional projects, such as dams. It would also include, however, newer types of power generation, such as wind power and sun power. The need for more power that is environmentally safe and efficient is key to the continuance of a functioning economy. It is worth emphasizing that all sectors would have to provide training for employees as necessary.

A fourth public agency would be AmeriEducate. This would employ qualified people and give human resources to public education at all levels from kindergarten to graduate education. Of course, each school or university would have to decide what type of job someone was qualified to do. It would include staff and faculty, but could also include construction workers directly or through contractors at the state or federal level.

One problem for this approach to employment is that it will take careful planning to ensure that every job offered is a necessary and useful job for society, not just a make-work activity. This means that even if the program were adopted right now, it would take some time to plan useful jobs for the millions of people now unemployed.

Each of the areas suggested above—infrastructure, education, health, and clean power—is vital to society. Finding the best projects within those areas, however, would take time. The only way to meet this problem for the future is to have the jobs all planned and ready whenever they are needed.

Congress and the president would, of course, examine the new proposals of these agencies every year. They could then change the emphasis, add, or subtract from them. The important point is that these agencies would always be ready to furnish new, useful jobs whenever unemployment might appear.

Conservatives will argue that public jobs will crowd out private ones. The public option for jobs, however, would only operate if there were unemployment because there are no private jobs available. The public employment would stimulate the economy and lay the foundation for more private jobs.

Another conservative argument against a public option for employment is the cost. The cost to government is, however, reduced by the ending of the need for unemployment compensation. The fact that people are doing useful jobs means that government is saved the money of paying for this job in some other program. Moreover, the fact that the expenditure stimulates a weak economy means that there is net gain for society.

If more government money is initially needed, it can be obtained by cutting military spending. The United States is currently fighting two wars to maintain its occupation of foreign countries, for six years in Iraq and for eight years in Afghanistan. A widespread view in the rest of the world says that the main point of both wars has been to expand American power and to make the whole Middle East region safe for the profit-making activities of the giant global corporations. When the troops are all withdrawn from Iraq and Afghanistan by Nobel Peace Prize winner Barack Obama, there will be more than enough money for the public options for health care and full employment.

A stimulus plan that is designed to stimulate private production may allow private companies to find ways to expand production with little or no increase in employment. A public option for employment is the only way to ensure rapid recovery of employment from recession-caused unemployment. Only a permanent public option can ensure that mass unemployment never happens again. Unemployment is a painful disease of modern capitalist society, a disease that must be eliminated.

## Global Action

The economic crisis of 2007 to 2009 was a global crisis. Measures paralleling those discussed above need application on the global scale. Details of global proposals and plausible ways to fight for them as well as enforce them would take another entire book. This is a project for the future.

## Conclusion

This book has solved the question of why expansions always end up in recessions in the roller coaster economy called capitalism. The most basic institutions of that economy cause the jaws of a nutcracker to close on profits at the end of the expansion. Aspects of this economic structure worsened over many decades and led to a housing crisis, a financial crisis, and the deepest recession since the Great Depression, with the longest and strongest unemployment. The only way to end the business cycle of boom and bust is to make drastic enough changes in the institutions that lead to the roller coaster economy.

Financial regulations are important. Even if the strongest regulations, however, are passed and enforced, they will only work to prevent financial crisis if there is first a structural change in banking and other financial corporations. The largest banks should pass from the private control of a few people, who make billions in profits, to the control of a democratically elected government.

GM should remain in public hands so that it can be the center of research and development on environmentally safe and efficient automobiles. Corporations that are "too big to fail" must be prevented from failing in a deep recession by public ownership.

Democratization also means replacing the broken health care system, in which the private insurance companies control everything and make ever-increasing profits, while increasing numbers of people are uninsured. The broken health care system should be replaced by a new one in which the private plans must compete with a public plan, giving people a public option for their health.

A democratic society must also replace the ailing economic system of private companies that fire millions of employees in every recession. There must be a public option of employment at reasonable wages and salaries, doing vital public jobs, guaranteed to every unemployed American.

Unfortunately, reality must be admitted. Reality says that the public options in both health care and employment have always been opposed by the enormous power of the largest corporations, who believe that public options for consumers and for employees may limit the companies' power to make billions and billions of dollars. Only a very strong public movement will pass legislation creating public options for health and jobs. Since human beings made the economic institutions causing the business cycle, human beings can change them. If politicians will enact the program given above, including public options for health and jobs, then people without health insurance can get public health insurance, while people without jobs can get jobs in the public sector. It is a simple question of social engineering.

## Suggested Readings

There is an outstanding, detailed paper by eighteen authors, called "A Progressive Program for Economic Recovery and Financial Reconstruction." The website and all the authors' names are given in the References section (see Balakrishnan et al. 2009).

An extremely clear article is Robert Pollin's "How to End the Recession" (2008b). There are three comprehensive and advanced articles on a full employment plan: Thomas Palley, "Government as Employer of Last Resort" (2001); Malcolm Sawyer, "Employer of Last Resort" (2003); and Randall Wray, "Government as Employer of Last Resort" (1997).

The relationship of democratic political institutions to capitalist economic institutions is best described in Samuel Bowles and Herbert Gintis's *Democracy and Capitalism* (1986). Their point is that democratic economic institutions are necessary not only for economic stability, but also for a firm basis to political democracy.

The development of employees' cooperatives is told with excellent scholarship in Christopher Gunn's *Workers' Self-Management in the United States* (1984). Gunn followed up with a book covering nonprofit enterprises as well as cooperatives, *Third Sector Development* (2004). The vehement arguments for and against a system of cooperative enterprises are presented clearly by Robin Hahnel in *Economic Justice and Democracy* (2005).

# References

Adler, Stephen. 2008. "Will We Ever Learn?" *Business Week*, September 18. www.businessweek.com/magazine/content/08_39/b4101016034380. htm?chan=magazine+channel_the+business+week.

Aldcroft, Derek H. 1993. *The European Economy, 1914–1990*. 3rd ed. London: Routledge.

Balakrishnan, Radhika, James Crotty, Edwin Dickens, Gerald Epstein, Thomas Ferguson, Teresa Ghilarducci, Jo-Marie Greisgraber, Stephany Griffith-Jones, Robert Guttmann, Arjun Jayadev, Anush Kapadia, David Kotz, Michael Meerepol, Fred Moseley, Jose Antonio Ocampo, Robert Pollin, Malcolm Sawyer, and Martin Wolfson. 2009. "A Progressive Program for Economic Recovery and Financial Reconstruction." Political Economy Research Institute, University of Massachusetts Amherst, January 1. www.peri.umass. edu/fileadmin/pdf/other_publication_types/PERI_SCEPA_statementJan27.pdf.

Bowles, Samuel, and Herbert Gintis. 1986. *Democracy and Capitalism: Property, Community, and the Contradictions of Modern Social Thought*. New York: Basic Books.

Bregger, John E., and Steven E. Haugen. 1995. "BLS Introduces New Range of Alternative Unemployment Measures." *Monthly Labor Review*, October.

Brenner, Harvey. 1976. "Estimating the Social Costs of National Economic Policy: Implications for Mental Health and Criminal Aggression." U.S. Congress, Joint Economic Committee, 94th Cong, 2nd Sess. Washington, DC: U.S. Government Printing Office.

Bureau of Economic Analysis (BEA), U.S. Department of Commerce. www.bea.gov.

Burns, Arthur F., and Wesley C. Mitchell. 1946. "Measuring Business Cycles." In *Studies in Business Cycles*, No. 2. New York: National Bureau of Economic Research.

Carroll, Lewis. 1901. *Alice's Adventures in Wonderland*. Boston: DeWolfe, Fiske.

Cole, H.L., and L.E. Ohanian. 2004. "New Deal Policies and the Persistence of the Great Depression: A General Equilibrium Analysis." *Journal of Political Economy* 112: 779–816.

Cooper, Michael. 2008. "McCain Advisor Refers to 'Nation of Whiners.'" *New York Times*, July 11. www.nytimes.com/2008/07/11/us/politics/11campaign.html.

Duggan, Marie. 2009. "The Specter of Capital Flight: How Long Will the Power of the Dollar Protect the U.S.?" *Dollars & Sense*, January–February. www.dollarsandsense. org/archives/2009/0109duggan.html.

Federal Reserve System, Board of Governors. www.federalreserve.gov.

Friedman, Milton, and Anna Schwartz. 1971. *A Monetary History of the United States, 1867–1960*. Princeton, NJ: Princeton University Press.

# REFERENCES

Galbraith, John Kenneth. 1988. *The Great Crash, 1929*. New York: Houghton-Mifflin.

Greenspan, Alan. 2008. Testimony, Committee of Government Oversight and Reform, October 23. http://oversight.house.gov/documents/20081023100438.pdf.

Gunn, Christopher. 1984. *Workers' Self-Management in the United States*. Ithaca, NY: Cornell University Press.

————. 2004. *Third Sector Development: Making Up for the Market*. Ithaca, NY: Cornell University Press.

Hahnel, Robin. 2005. *Economic Justice and Democracy: From Competition to Cooperation*. New York: Routledge.

Hall, Robert, et al. 2003. "The NBER's Recession Dating Procedure." National Bureau of Economic Research, October 21. www.nber.org/cycles/recessions.html.

Jenkins, Holman W., Jr. 2008. "How to Shake Off the Mortgage Mess." *Wall Street Journal*, July 30. http://online.wsj.com/article/SB121737434767195077.html?mod=todays _columnists.

Leonhardt, David. 2009. "A Bold Plan Sweeps Away Reagan Ideas." *New York Times*, February 26. www.nytimes.com/2009/02/27/business/economy/27policy.html.

Lifsher, Marc, and Alana Semuels. 2009. "Job Losses Mount Among California Government Workers." *Los Angeles Times*, July 18.

Magdoff, Harry. 2003. *Imperialism Without Colonies*. New York: Monthly Review Press.

Miller, John. 2005. "Dollar Anxiety." *Dollars & Sense*, January–February. www. dollarsandsense.org/archives/2005/0105miller.html.

Mitchell, Wesley C. 1951. *What Happens During Business Cycles: A Progress Report*. New York: National Bureau of Economic Research.

Mitchell, Wesley C., and W.L. Thorp. 1926. *Business Annals*. New York: National Bureau of Economic Research.

National Bureau of Economic Research (NBER). 2008. "Determination of the 2007 Peak in Economic Activity." Business Cycle Dating Committee. December 11. www.nber .org/cycles/dec2008.html.

————. 2009. "Business Cycle Expansions and Contractions." www.nber.org/cycles/.

Palley, Thomas I. 2001. "Government as Employer of Last Resort: Can It Work?" In *53rd Annual Proceedings, Industrial Relations Research Association*, 269–274.

Pollin, Robert. 2004. *Contours of Descent: U.S. Economic Fractures and the Landscape of Global Austerity*. New York: Verso.

————. 2007. "Global Outsourcing and the U.S. Working Class." *New Labor Forum* 16 (1): 122–125.

————. 2008a. "The Housing Bubble and Financial Deregulation: Isn't Enough Enough?" *New Labor Forum* 17 (2): 118–121.

————. 2008b. "How to End the Recession." *The Nation*, November 24, 13–16.

Reagan, Ronald. 1982. "The President's News Conference." January 19. www.reagan .utexas.edu/archives/speeches/1982/11982b.htm.

Sawyer, Malcolm. 2003. "Employer of Last Resort: Could It Deliver Full Employment and Price Stability?" *Journal of Economic Issues* 37 (4): 881–908.

Scannell, Kara, and Sudeep Reddy. 2008. "Greenspan Admits Errors to Hostile House Panel." *Wall Street Journal*, October 24. http://online.wsj.com/article /SB122476545437862295.html.

Sherk, James. 2009. "Rising Unemployment: Caused by Less New Job Creation, Not by More Layoffs." *Backgrounder*, January 6.

Sherman, Howard J. 1991. *The Business Cycle: Growth and Crisis Under Capitalism*. Princeton, NJ: Princeton University Press.

————. 2001. "The Business Cycle Theory of Wesley Mitchell." *Journal of Economic Issues* 35 (1): 85–97.

———— 2003. "Institutions and the Business Cycle." *Journal of Economic Issues* (3): 621–642.

————. 2006. *How Society Makes Itself: The Evolution of Political and Economic Institutions.* Armonk, NY: M.E. Sharpe.

Sherman, Howard J., E.K. Hunt, Reynold F. Nesiba, Phillip A. O'Hara, and Barbara Wiens-Tuers. 2008. *Economics: An Introduction to Traditional and Progressive Views.* Armonk, NY: M.E. Sharpe.

Spirer, Herbert, Louise Spirer, and A.J. Jaffe. 1998. *Misused Statistics.* New York: Marcel Dekker.

Stein, Sam. 2008. "McCain on 'Black Monday': Fundamentals of Our Economy Are Still Strong." *Huffington Post*, September 15. www.huffingtonpost.com/2008/09/15/mccain-fundamentals-of-th_n_126445.html.

Terkel, Studs. 1970. *Hard Times: An Oral History of the Great Depression.* New York: Pantheon Books.

Towns, Edolphus. 2008. "Committee Holds Hearing on the Role of Federal Regulators in the Financial Crisis." Committee on Oversight and Government Reform, 111th Congress of the United States, October 23.

Valletta, Rob. 2005. "Help-Wanted Advertising and Job Vacancies." *Federal Reserve Bank of San Francisco Economic Letter*, no. 2 (January 21), 1–3. www.frbsf.org/publications /economics/letter/2005/el2005–02.html.

Volcker, Paul. www.huffingtonpost.com/2009/04/23/volcker-us-world-in-a-gre_n_190761 .html.

Wray, L. Randall. 1997. "Government as Employer of Last Resort: Full Employment Without Inflation." Levy Economics Institute Working Paper No. 213, November.

# Index

# About the Author

**Howard J. Sherman** was chair of Economics at the University of California, Riverside, for five years. He has published 20 books and over 100 articles. His books include *The Business Cycle: Growth and Crisis Under Capitalism* (1991). He also has published *How Society Makes Itself: The Evolution of Political and Economic Institutions* (M.E. Sharpe 2005).